# A Lunch Line

**Contemporary Scenes
for Contemporary Teens**

by Caleen Jennings

**New Plays Incorporated, Box 371, Bethel, CT 06801**

New Plays Incorporated
P.O. Box 5074
Charlottesville, VA 22905

# CONTENTS

# Acknowledgements

Thanks to Julian Mayfield who told me, "If you want to write, read!" Thanks to Gerry Schoenfeld who showed me there's poetry in everything — even ad copy! Thanks to Niamani and Ishan, who staged my first play. Thanks to my inspirational teachers Murray Lewis, John Gillespie, Paul Grey, Victor Bumbalo, Judy Dunn, Alice Spivak, Olympia Dukakis, Peter Kass, Omar Shapli, and Lowell Swortzell. Thanks to the Bethesda Acadmy: to all my talented and eager students, to my creative and supportive colleagues and to Executive Director Bonnie Fogel, who gets my work funded and seen. Thanks to Valerie Morris, Gail Breeskin and the theatre faculty at The American University for expanding my artistic horizons. Thanks to the students and faculty of Lynnbrook, Karma House and Caithness Shelter — my toughest yet most trusting and risk- taking group to date. Thanks to all the students and parent supporters in my own theatre group: Black Kids in Theatre. Thanks to my parents, Calvin and Elinor Sinnette, who made me read, showed me the world, paid for me to learn juggling and improvisation when I should have been earning a living — and still believed in me. Thanks to Tante who was my Mom away from home and who talked me out of go-go dancing. Thanks to Dee, Jerry and Lucas for their laughter and love when I need it the most. My deepest, heartfelt thanks to my children Robeson and DuBois, who forgave my late nights and whose precious beauty and shining spirits keep me young at heart. To my husband Carl: I love you. You've always told me I could write and direct and never said, "I told you so" when I finally did. You've always forced me to go further and be better than I thought I could be. You've always told me frankly if my work stinks, and praised me as if I am capable of perfection. And to my innovative, adventurous publisher, Pat Whitton, who said, "These scenes don't fit into any category. I like that."

# DIRECTING SCENES WITH TEENAGERS

I wonder how many of you who work with young performers have found yourselves in the same situation I encountered in March, 1986. I had had years of intense training as an actress, but never in my wildest dreams did I think I'd end up teaching children, much less writing for young people's theatre. Suddenly, there I was standing in a classroom, face to face with ten very serious, very talented, very young students who wanted to do monologues and scenes. None of the material I came across seemed appropriate for them. Most plays hinged around a single star. What to do with the nine other kids in the class? Existing scenes were either on the level of Dick and Jane or *A Streetcar Named Desire,* with little or no middle ground. What to do with kids who were still kids, but who wanted more meaty, substantive pieces with real drama and conflict?

As every teacher knows — when you don't have what you need, make it up! Almost casually, I set out to create some pieces that would highlight the children's individual talents and provide me with a good vehicle for directing, as well as teaching acting, voice and diction. I discovered I thoroughly enjoy writing for young performers. I have been doing it steadily for the past three years.

Here, then, is a collection of scenes I have written specifically for students I have worked with throughout the D.C. metropolitan area. The teens who have performed them have been urban and suburban; black, white, Hispanic and Asian; wealthy and economically disadvantaged; well-adjusted and not. My point is that teens of all colors, cultures and economic backgrounds have something in common: adolescence. It is my hope that these scenes will, in some small way, help them through it.

## How to Use This Book

I hope these scenes and monologues will serve as:

. A collection of age appropriate material for boys and girls between twelve and eighteen (or even as young as ten in some cases)

. A point of discussion relevant to today's children, dealing with topics such as parent/child relationships, school, friendship, race, class and gender issues

. Inspiration for those of you who are homeroom, English or social studies teachers, camp directors, recreational aides or the unlucky soul who got stuck with coming up with a 45 minute assembly piece. I hope that the notes I've written about the scenes, from creation to production, will inspire you to create your own scripts for your own performers. Nothing would give me greater pleasure than knowing that I had convinced some of my readers to set out on this challenging, gratifying, enriching adventure.

I have tried to include a wide range of scenes dealing with themes relevant to adolescents. You may want to use them in a number of ways:

. As a classroom project, concentrating on the literary side: what makes drama; what is conflict; the nature of dialogue and how it differs from narrative; character traits, etc.

. You may wish to stage the scenes for classroom use only, concentrating on the process of acting, ensemble play, listening, movement, and speaking in front of a group.

. Or you may wish to take several scenes and put them together for a program, in class or in the auditorium (cafeteria, all purpose room, etc.) to which you invite an audience.

The scenes in this book are written for all kinds of teens in different combinations. There are girl-girl scenes for two or more characters, boy-boy scenes for two or more chacters, and a few boy-girl scenes. Some, with a culture- specific theme or plot, are written specifically for black performers, but most are written for performers of any and all colors, cultural or ethnic backgrounds, sizes, shapes and personalities.

## Making Changes to Suit Your Needs

Depending upon the composition of your group, you may have to change the gender of some of the characters. When doing this, you may want to look for scenes/monologues where the themes and actions are less gender-specific. The scene "Beautiful" from *The Only One Who Knows* deals specifically with a boy's reaction to a girl and would require a lot of re- writing. On the other hand a monologue like "The Big A" or a scene like "Leaving" would require very little or no rewriting. Go over the scenes in advance and make your decisions about casting and rewriting. Your students may have good insights about how to rewrite and reshape characters to accommodate gender changes.

These scenes have been written in 1988 and 1989. Much has changed, and that's the understatement of the century! Teenager's interests change rapidly. What was cool in 1986 may be unknown today. Slang and other turns of phrase will have to be updated. Students love to assist in these kinds of changes. Rely on them to tell you what's correct and incorrect in these scenes. Ask them to help you update the language and make it appropriate to their social, cultural norms. It's a great opportunity for sharing as well as getting assistance with script rewrites.

## Working with Teens

It's not everybody's cup of tea, but I happen to love working with middle school/high school students. If the essence of drama is conflict, what stage of life could possibly be more suited to the study of drama than adolescence? It's a stage fraught with contradictions: high energy vs. incredible lethargy; rebelliousness vs. conformity; fear of failure vs. bold, sometimes even foolhardy risk-taking. Adolescence is a battlefield upon which the adult parts and the child parts of the individual go at it 'round the clock. Performers at this age summon up tremendous courage getting up on stage in front of peers and parents. The performance experience for this age group, when designed and supervised by empathic, energetic teachers, can be a formidable rite of passage, the just rewards being a tangible boost in self-confidence and adult and peer group affirmation.

It's a curse and a blessing that I have incredibly vivid memories of my own adolescence: a curse in that my hormonal turmoil and general awkwardness with life at that age are conditions I would prefer to permanently forget; a blessing in that I draw upon my own experiences to create scenes. It has been gratifying to have adolescents say to me, "Gee, how did you know about that? That's just like what happened to me one time."

***Observing.*** But heaven knows that the late 80's are a far cry from the late 60's when I was a teen. I have to be careful to keep in tune and keep current if my material is to ring true. I do this by observing the students I teach. These observations are completely informal — in the hallway, on breaks, on the bus, overhearing snatches of conversations in the cafeteria or in the girls' bathroom. I want to see how they group themselves and interact. I want to hear kids being themselves, talking about the things that matter to them. I must be careful to keep adult/parental judgements out of it. For instance, as a parent of a pre-teen, I find the whole

2

designer jeans phenomenom ridiculous. As a writer, I find it a veritable gold mine of material. I'm constantly seeking to strike a balance between representing the phenomenon from a student's perspective, and challenging it with adult insights, values, and, I hope, wisdom. I'm not above slipping in a message now and then, if I can do it respectfully and subtly. At least, that's my goal.

*Discussing.* In developing material, it is extremely useful to have group discussions about various issues in students' lives. It was tremendous fun for me to pull out a big sheet of newsprint, write "PARENTS" across the top, and make two columns underneath — "PROS" and "CONS." Not only did I get 45 minutes of the liveliest, most exciting discussion ever, but it also generated oodles of raw material for improvisations and scenes as we explored issues such as popularity, sibling rivalry, peer pressure, stress, dating, friendships and related topics.

Use the scenes as a point of discussion. Read a scene, then ask your students questions like these:

. What point do you think the author was trying to make?
. Did she make the point realistically?
. Which character, if any, is right? Which character is wrong?
. Are any of the situations or characters familiar to you?
. In what way?
. If you had to write a different ending, what would it be?
. What would these characters be doing if they were not here talking to each other?
. Describe the home life of each of these characters — what their parents are like, how many in the family, grades, social life, day dreams, what he/she will be like at age 40.
. If you could cast this scene with film or television celebrities, who would play each part? How did you come to make those selections?

Students often answer questions about characters highly autobiographically, thus giving real insight into their own feelings, attitudes and beliefs.

*Listening.* Above all, LISTEN TO YOUR STUDENTS. Create the kind of safe environment in which students can talk about and demonstrate their ideas. As a teacher, playwright and director, you must listen non-judgementally. Demonstrate that you respect and value your students' ideas. Put your concerns about grammar, posture, tidiness aside for the time being. That's not to say that all ground rules for classroom behavior go out of the window. Far from it. I believe that the environment must be structured and disciplined. The main thing is to show your students that you value their ideas and creativity, that you appreciate hearing their points of view.

## Ground Rules for Rehearsing

There's a long-standing, and to my mind destructive and dangerous myth that acting/creative dramatics for children and youth is "run around and do whatever you want to express yourself" time. Not in my classes. I believe in structure and discipline. My motto is, "Be cheerful, but firm." Within the boundaries of acceptable social interaction, there is ultimate freedom. Make it clear that rules must be adhered to for the safety and well-being of the ensemble.

Develop your own set of ground rules for improvisation and ensemble activity. Preferably,

3

generate these on the blackboard as a group. Rely on the students to develop, agree to and follow their own code of behavior. Points which should emerge include these:

. Every performer deserves quiet attention when on the stage. When an actor is performing, there must be absolute quiet, with attention focused on stage.

. We all know the difference between laughing supportively and laughing derisively. Only the former is allowed.

. All ideas and creative suggestions are worthy of respect. Decisions must benefit the group as a whole.

. When the teacher/leader says "Cut" or "Freeze" all action is to STOP AT ONCE.

. No physical contact between actors. Find other ways to express whatever emotions arise in the scene. Use objects to express your emotions, not your classmates.

. The teacher/leader will seek, even rely on student input. However, all final decisions rest with the leader.

. The same rules for classroom behavior apply to ensemble acting behavior. No foul language nor references to sex, drugs or alcohol.

. Tasks such as arriving promptly at rehearsals, learning lines, bringing in props will be mutually agreed upon and adhered to.

## Organizing

Teachers/leaders, organize,plan, prepare. Know what you're dealing with in terms of:

. Developmental, educational, and social levels of your students. Ask yourself if the scene(s) are appropriate to this group. Will you be able to include everyone in the class on some level?

. Main objectives you want to accomplish. What do you wish the students and the audience to come away with in the end? What do you, personally, wish to accomplish through this activity?

. Support network. Are there others you can depend on? Fellow teachers? Administration? Parents? Mature students?

. Physical environment — assets and liabilities of classroom, stage, outdoor or other performance areas.

. Resources — ordering scripts, photocopying (with attendant copyright and royalty concerns), props, sets, tickets, etc.

. Performance date. Develop a rehearsal and performance schedule that is realistic.

## Selecting Material — Improvisation vs. Scripts

Many of my colleagues work successfully with teens using improvisation as both the means and the end. There is no doubt that improvising in performance, when done well, is an exhilarating walk along the edge of the razor blade, calling for keen ensemble play, quick thinking and advanced level performance skills, particularly in the area of vocal projection and articulation. These colleagues never have to nag students to memorize their lines or be true to the playwright's words, for they are creating the scene live and in real time.

While I find improvisations an invaluable tool in the creation of material, I am a confirmed believer in the value of scripted material for several reasons. First and foremost, it is a permanent record of what has been created, shaped and solidified by the group. It may be treasured and passed along to other groups. If the script is collaborative or written from improvisations, it is tremendously gratifying and confirming for a student to see his/her work in written form.

Secondly, acting from a script requires reading skills — from basic comprehension to advanced inferential and interpretive abilities. I have found performance to be a wonderful motivator for students to improve reading skills and build their vocabularies. Reading a script and discussing characters provides a great opportunity to explore such things as synonyms, connotation and denotation, vernacular, beginning-middle-end, narration, dialogue, description. An educator should take advantage of every opportunity to reinforce the power of the written word. The word is insight into the mind of the creator: the themes, situations, characters, actions in the scene. The word is an actor's most valuable tool in completing the action and releasing the emotion.

## Creating Your Own Material

You may want to consider the scenes in this book as springboards to your original scenes. You and your students will invest so much more in a project that is completely original.

For example, using the earlier discussion questions, you may ask students to improvise new scenes based on the action, stituations, themes and characters of the scenes in this book. Here are some starters:

*Action Improvisation.* What are these characters trying to do in this scene? (e.g., settle a dispute, start a fight, come out on top, show off, etc.) How else might they do it? Suppose they were both shy or depressed or angry, how would this change the action? What would they do differently?

*Situation Improvisation.* Take the same characters in this scene and put them in a new scene: Thanksgiving dinner. How would they behave? Would they help serve? Would they eat a lot, talk a lot, hide, start fights, giggle and act silly, feel shy, get sick?

*Theme Improvisation.* Take the theme of this scene and come up with two new characters in a different setting. Improvise a scene with the same theme

*Character Improvisation.* List three main personality traits for each character. Now let's set them in a similar scene at age 7, 25, 40, 60. Let's see these personality traits at each age.

Viola Spolin's *Improvisation* can help you construct improvisations to maximize the performance and script value.

Finding material is easy to do. If you have access to the students you have access to more inspiration than you'll know what to do with. Throw out questions. Challenge them. Ask them to act out typical parental behavior. Ask them to act out typical teen behavior. Ask them to act out how they are going to behave with their teenage kids when they get to be in their 30's and 40's. Create situations with problems, conflicts and obstacles built in. Allow the students to explore them verbally and in improvisations.

Ask your studentswhat topics interest them. Read a play (or poem or novel for that matter), isolate key themes and have students create a contemporary scene or play based on the same themes. Have students create alternate endings to scenes, invent new characters and create "spin off" scenes. Take a Shakespearean scene and have students set it in the 80's in a high school cafeteria. The possibilities are endless. Being educators, use all of your innate creativity to stimulate students and generate scenes and other performance material.

# Casting

Once you have the material for a performance, whether these scenes, originals or a combination of both, consider the casting. My scenes have been written to give all characters a moment in the spotlight. It's important to me, as I think it should be to anyone who teaches children and teens, to avoid the star syndrome. How much better to do a play with ten scenes around a given theme, in which everyone has an equal number of lines, a time to shine in the spotlight.

When casting, be aware of the experience you want each student to have playing his or her role. I've often cast the class whiner as a whiner in the scene. Of course I do this subtlely, without revealing my motives. What is amazing is that I have found that once given permission to be a no-holds-barred whiner on stage, the student generally stops doing it in class. I've also found this true in typecasting bullies, know-it-alls, prima donnas and introverts. Thus, by taking what may be problem behavior in class to the extreme on stage, the student often gets a new perspective on his/her behavior and makes changes for the better.

Consider also casting against type. I've had great success taking the class bully and casting himm as a wimp, or casting the shyest girl in the class as most popular girl. These students get to walk a mile in someone else's shoes, and the result is often that they discover new areas of their own personalities. Besides, it's just plain fun to play someone completely opposite to who you are. That's the joy of acting.

Sometimes I let students cast themselves. I let them decide who they want to work with and set everything up independently of me. In other instances, where I want to build group interaction, I cast students with classmates they do not know or have little interaction with. Rehearsal and performance experience is a great opportunity for social interaction and team building.

# Theatre Skills

Depending on their maturity and sophistication, you may wish to acquaint your students with some basic theatre concepts. The creative teacher/leader will find a subtle way to slip these into the work, make these skills seem grown-up and important and, better yet, fun.

Some of the basic skills students should be acquainted with and/or begin to develop are:

### Finding the action in the words.

The scenes in this book rely on the words to reveal plot, action and character. There are few to no stage directions. Rather, teacher/leaders and students will find the plot, actions, and clues to character in the words. To give you an example, here is a passage from the scene, "Tell Herman":

**Jean:**        You just finding that out? The little rich girl makes a discovery. Don't worry, honey, you'll get over it. Your life will go on. You'll grow up here in Ellenwood in your pretty clothes in your pretty room, snuggling up to big soft teddy bears and pigging out on 17 flavors of Baskin Robbins. By this time next year, you won't even remember my face.

6

There are no stage directions in this speech. What can we tell about the action from the words?

. **Plot.** (What is happening in the scene?) Jean is getting ready to leave and is preparing Sarah for her departure. She reminds Sarah of life's bitter realities, that life is not fair. She's telling Sarah that her life won't be affected in the long run, that her comfortable life will continue long after Jean's gone.

. **Action.** (What is Jean doing?) Jean gets tough with Sarah. She mocks her for being rich and naive. She points out Sarah's luxuries and puts down her comfortable existence. Jean challenges Sarah to even remember her in a year.

. **Character.** (How does Jean do it?) Jean uses sarcasm. She tries to shake up Sarah. Jean appears to be a tough kid who's seen a lot of the world. She has little faith in people and can't tolerate naive or spoiled behavior.

Looking at these elements, then, what can the student actor do to interpret and play the part? Ask your students:

. Look at the list of actions. Do they suggest blocking and movement in the scene?
. How do you think Jean moves her body when when she gets tough?
. How would she relate to Sarah physically? Would she touch her?
. Would Jean yell, or be very quietly angry?
. How would Jean's voice sound when she's being sarcastic?
. Would she put Sarah down in the mean way or in a sad, depressed way?

Show students that people never just talk to be talking. There's always a reason to speak. The words always represent an action the character is completing. Sometimes it's a physical action: e.g., Jean moves towards her, Jean shakes her. Sometimes it's a mental action: Jean mocks Sarah; Jean challenges her to remember her in a year.

Teens have an instinct for understanding action, but often feel shy to act on their instincts. This kind of script analysis is often helpful to get them out of a monotone. Point out the conflict, get the character physicalized and energized. Stanislavski's *An Actor Prepares* and Rockwood's *The Craftsmen of Dionysus* give excellent accounts of how to find the action in the text, and you may wish to do some selected reading in preparation to working with students.

### Concentration and Focus

These are the abilities to stay in character, focus on one's partner in the scene and the action of the scene. Viola Spolin's book, **Improvisation** has excellent exercises to build concentration and focus skills. Concentration and focus also imply the ability to sit quietly when not onstage, to behave in a manner that supports the group, the teacher/leader, and the project as a whole.

### Stage Movement

Young people need a basic understanding of how to face the audience and keep the body turned outward (certainly never turning a back to the audience), and following the blocking (pattern of stage movement) agreed to. That is, if it is established that Jean moves towards

Sarah on the line, "You just finding that out?" then the actress must do that realistically and consistently in rehearsal and performance. Have a stage manager keep a record of blocking, and make students write it in their scripts. They will forget it otherwise.

## Character Physicality

What does the way the character stands and moves say about his/her inner state and personality? Teens tend to slouch and vacillate between lethargy and hyperactivity. Let them explore the character on a physical level, and let the character traits indicate new ways of walking, sitting, picking up the phone, etc.

To go back to the scene, "Tell Herman," ask your student actress:

. How would Jean hold her shoulders?

. How would she hold her head?

. What would inside her tummy feel like?

. What would her face look like when she's mocking Sarah?

Remind students that these characters are not just talking heads; they are whole people. You as a teacher/leader may have to do some physical relaxation, loosening up and energizing exercises to get your student actors in touch with their bodies.

## Vocal Qualities, Volume and "Projection"

I put the word "projection" in quotation marks because I dislike the thought of "throwing the voice." What's really being referred to is volume, and teachers of kids and teens know the endless nagging: "We can't hear you! Speak louder!" It's a gutsy adult, much less a kid, who can stand up on stage in front of adults and peers to speak at full volume. Teacher/leaders need to be sensitive to this, while at the same time serving the purpose at hand: getting the play heard!

It is important to remember that voice is RELEASE, not tension. We want to release the breath, the words, the thought. Not push or strain. I like to stand in back of the room and ask my students, "How would you call me if I was your best friend on the other side of the cafeteria during lunch time, with 300 other kids in there?" After they've each demonstrated, using my name, I ask them to go back and take a couple of lines from the scene, using that same volume. Then I ask them to keep the same volume while making it conversational, in character, consistent with what is happening in the scene. I use my hand as a kind of meter. Whenever volume drops, my hand goes up in the back of the room.

It's the idea of including the room in a conversation rather than shouting or straining. This awareness of volume should begin on day one of rehearsal. Don't let kids rehearse for days and weeks at an inaudible level and expect them to pump it up magically for performance. Quite the contrary, you can count on the volume dropping dramatically during performance, out of anxiety, self-consciousness . . . whatever. So make volume awareness a continuous part of the rehearsal process.

Kristin Linklater's book, **Freeing the Natural Voice** and Jon Eisenson's book, **Voice and Diction** will provide you with some solid insights and exercises to build basic vocal skills for performance.

## Rate

Almost every adolescent I know reads lines as if on a speeding locomotive. Words tumble out so fast it's almost impossible to understand and follow what's being said. This is often because lines are memorized at this rate, sped through over and over with no thought to meaning, action, character. One of the most effective ways I've found in dealing with this problem is borrowed from a wonderful voice and diction teacher of mine, Ms. Nora Dunfee. Whenever meaning got lost in a reading, she would simply and pleasantly interrupt with a question. "Which?" "When?" "How?" "What?" "Where?" We had to respond to her using the line of dialogue in question. Sometimes she'd ask the same question three or four times, until the actor's line reading indicated intent, intelligence, meaning, feeling. I always explain what I'm doing when I use this technique, and lavish praise when the meaning clicks. Working through a speech in this way tends to re-focus the actor on the action in the scene — what he/she is really saying and doing with the words. If real attention is being paid, the rate will generally slow down.

## Diction

Teens are notorious mumblers. Rather than coming on with the "how-now-brown-cow" approach, show students how the emotions come out of the words. Again, words are the actor's best friend. To go back to our character Jean, imagine how she would say, "The little rich girl makes a discovery." She's being sarcastic. She's using the words as a weapon. Tell your actress to make the words crisp and pointed, use the words to dig at Sarah. It's almost impossible to do that with a lazy tongue or a mouth that's not open wide enough. The other technique I've found useful is to audio-tape students. They are often out of touch with how garbled they sound. Reinforce the fact that they are aiming for maximum clarity for the audience, not to alter their own speech patterns. Teens are often afraid that you'll turn them into "nerds" by having them articulate clearly. Make it clear this is just for the performance and that mumbling's still great for dates and parties and hanging out. It's just inappropriate for an audience who wants to know what's going on.

## Memorization

There's no one right and perfect way to memorize. I have found it useful to ask students to examine their own learning styles in order to develop the best individual approach. (This is a highly simplistic incorporation of neuro- linguistic programming (NLP). After years of wondering why some kids just couldn't memorize or listen, I have found it successful):

. Those who are **visually** oriented may need to see the words over and over again while saying them aloud. They may want to make giant cue cards or use newsprint to help them see large and remember.

. Those who are **auditory** learners often benefit from having their lines said to them and repeating them, or even better, using a tape recorder. To use the tape recorder, have the scene partner read his/her lines onto a tape, leaving a space where the other partner's lines come. That partner then rehearses the scene with the tape recorder as his partner. Or have the student tape his/her own lines and listen to them over and over again.

. Those who are **kinesthetically** oriented (touching/moving kinds of kids) need to memorize lines with blocking and physical action. In that way they attach the words to something they do physically. For instance, every time he/she says, "I don't think you understand," they brush back their hair, or when they say the line "I think you're funny," they smile. Connect the words with something tangible and physical. (Don't go to extremes, however. You obviously don't want excessive moving and twitching.

The worst thing a student can do in memorizing is run lines in a locomotive speed monotone. That's just how he/she will perform it. Memorize with all the action, feeling, emphasis, character behavior that you will show in performance.

### Ensemble Skills (Getting Along, Listening, Give and Take)

The cast of any play is a team. In any group of adolescents you will find cliques, arch rivalries, in- group/out-group phenomena. My approach is to tell students right off, "I'm not asking you to like one another. Your friends and your enemies are your own business. I absolutely require, however, that you work together to get this job done. You're going to have to find a way to work and interact with strangers and enemies as well as friends. In your scene, you may have to hold hands and be best friends with your deadliest enemy. You're going to have to find a way to make that scene 100% believable. That's your task as an actor."

Listening is essential, and that too is a skill. Teens often day dream and block out directions. I've found that having them repeat what I've said helps me stay sane. Listening is critical, of course, when taking direction and feedback. Keeping in mind that every individual receives information in different modes, again it may be useful to ask students how they work best. .

First ask students how they need to receive direction and feedback in order to really understand and internalize it. Ask if they follow it more clearly through seeing it, hearing it, or doing it. Then adjust your mode of giving feedback accordingly.

. To the **visually** oriented student (has to see the feedback in order to really understand it): "Would you like me to write out my notes (feedback) and give you a copy? That way you can see what needs work." Or "Let me demonstrate what I want you to do."

. To the **aurally** oriented student (Has to hear the feedback in order to really understand it): "Let me talk through my feedback with you. You listen and ask questions when you need to."

. To the **kinesthetically oriented student** (Has to move physically or touch in order to understand the feedback): "Let's walk through the scene together the way I want you to do it."

## The Quality of Leadership, Direction, Feedback

Directing students and giving them feedback in a performance environment follows the same basic principles you use in good classroom teaching:

### Be Sensitive

Remember that this is the age for peer consciousness and peer pressure. Make sure what you say to each individual is appropriate in a group setting. As teacher/leader, you're going to be under a lot of pressure. Keep a firm grip on your energy, patience, temper, nerves. Remember you must model the behavior you want in your performers.

Make sure the group understands that the rehearsal area has to be confidential and safe so that risk-taking may thrive. It is unacceptable to gossip about what goes on in rehearsal outside of the ensemble. Students must be supportive of each other.

### Be Positive

Find something encouraging to say. Praise improvement. Make sure everyone gets a dose of reinforcement.

### Be Clear

Communicate ground rules, standards of behavior and performance in a way that everyone understands. Make sure criticism/negative feedback is specific and behavior oriented. "You slur your words" may be valid feedback but the logical question that follows is, "So what do you want me to do about that?" Much better is to try to put that feedback in a positive, action-oriented behavioral context; e.g., "That's good, but this time see if you can open your mouth a little wider, make the words a little sharper and crisper." Demonstrate what you want if appropriate.

Set realistic expectations. Have the students contribute to that list of expectations so that everyone is working out of a common framework.

### Be Fair

Give everyone feedback. Students who are doing well and who are easy to work with need feedback just as much as your "problem students." Make sure you find time to give feedback to everyone.

If you do have problem students, set aside time outside of group time to work with them individually, rather than eating into ensemble time and slowing down the process.

Don't fall into the trap of playing favorites. It's always terribly obvious and eats into group morale. Give everyone attention and a chance to shine.

### Challenge Students

There is always more to learn. I haven't met a student yet who is without talent. There are simply different kinds. For every student, find a way to praise what is good, then set the next goal. Find a way to keep challenging the bright, talented, know-it-all types. Make it clear that there's no such thing as perfection. There's always the next rung to climb. That's true of the world's greatest actors and certainly of all of us.

### Be Consistent

It's hard for teens (any performer for that matter) to deal with change and/or uncertainty. Sure there will be things that do not work and must be changed. But try to keep these changes at a minimum, especially as you get closer to performance. This will put the burden on you as teacher/leader to be prepared well in advance, to have clear ideas, and to communicate clearly and finalize appropriately.

Beware of stagnation. You don't want things so set that they appear rote. You don't want performers sleep- walking through the show. You may need to give them new tidbits here and there to keep everyone energized and fresh. But major changes are difficult to accommodate. Should they be required, introduce them with sensitivity and work to help your performers accommodate them.

# Developing a Program

If you are adventurous, if your children are ready, or even if neither of the former apply but you've been ordered to, you may begin to construct a 30 to 60 minute program for performance. Some of the main questions to ask yourself are:

## *Scope of Project*

. How elaborate/simple do I want this program to be? What can I realistically handle? What can I realistically expect my students to handle? What facilities/resources/knowledge do I have to ensure successful completion of this project.

. What are my goals in staging this project? What do I hope to learn as a teacher/leader? What do I want my students to learn?

## *Budget*

. Do I have a budget? If not, how can my students and I utilize existing resources, construct what we need, and bring items from home?

. If we need funds, where can I get them? Administration? Voluntary contributions (from whom?) Fundraising? Who can help me get support on building a budget?

. If I plan to contribute out of pocket, what is my limit? Can I get reimbursement or tax credit?

## *Support*

. Do I as teacher/leader have the support of my administration, colleagues, parents and students in this venture? Can I rely on assistance in organization, stage managing, publicity?

## *Legal Obligations*

. Do I have the O.K. of my administration? Have I informed them of this project, gotten their input and authorization?

. Must I notify any other authorities?

. If using copyrighted material, have I made arrangements for royalties?

. Are there fire, public safety, parking, insurance regulations I must know about and follow?

## *Planning/Scheduling*

. How can I organize and prepare myself and my students and support people in advance?

. What timetable must I set for read-thrus, rehearsals, run-throughs, technical rehearsals (if any), open or closed dress rehearsal, and actual performance?

. What publicity must be developed, and when must posters and flyers be sent out to the school, parents, community and media?

. When must the program with cast list and acknowledgements be ready?

. What logistics must be worked out with the building maintenance staff, to set up and take down chairs, clean audience and playing area, move and remove sets? (GET THEM ON YOUR SIDE WAY IN ADVANCE. THEY ARE THE SOURCE OF MUCH HELPFUL INFORMATION.)

## Length of Program

. Who is my audience? Depending on their age range and maturity, 30 minutes might be preferable to 45 or 60 minutes.
. Can my students sustain performance energy for 45 to 60 minutes?
. Will the audience be comfortable for 60 minutes (particularly in a classroom)? Is there enough space and ventillation for them?

## Giving the Piece a Structure and a Rhythm

Try to avoid being predictable. How can you keep the audience energized? How can you surprise them? To maintain the audience and performers' interest levels, bring variety in

. **Content.** Try a combination of scenes, monologues, poetry, songs/music, dance rather than a series of scenes one after the other. Your goal is to stimulate as many senses as possible.
. **Visual.** Use colors, shapes, space, angles, light, textures, etc.
. **Pace.**) Vary comedy with serious scenes, male with female, slow with quick, loud with quiet scenes.

To tie the pieces of the show together for flow, consider music, or writing a narrative and using a storyteller/narrator.

## Playing Area and Sets

How can you maximize the available space? Can you use interesting angles? Can the performers use a prescribed playing area, move out into the audience, or a combination of both? Does the playing area ensure that everyone in the audience has an unobstructed view?

If you don't have access to sets (platforms, flats, furniture), what can you use from the school or bring from home which will serve as a set? My students and I have created surroundings for scenes from cardboard, egg crates, construction paper and pieces of fabric. The main requirement is to keep them functional but simple and easy to main and move.

Make sure the sets you use are well constructed, and wear- and accident-proof. A storage area ensures that sets are not damaged, stolen, or tampered with.

## Props, Make-Up and Costumes

Make a list of props that MUST be included in the scenes to enhance the realism and the action. Young actors like to use props, but they can be misused as well. If props take attention away from the scene, if they become busy-work and distract the actors, it's better to do without. My motto is, the simpler the better.

These scenes are written for teens in a naturalistic setting — i.e., as they are in everyday life. None require elaborate costumes. I have staged all of these with students wearing the same clothes they wear to school. The students were always disappointed, I might add. "Oh, Mrs. Jennings, I wanted to paint my eyelids silver! I wanted to wear a ball gown!" It's true that kids of all ages love to dress up. But the responsibility for make-up and props can be awesome.

My advice is to KEEP IT VERY SIMPLE, especially in your first efforts. I usually tell my students no additional make-up. Since they are playing kids similar to themselves, they should be on the same level in terms of make up and clothing. However, I tell them they may bring in ONE prop or costume accessory that's appropriate — e.g., a show-off type character may bring in a long flowing scarf or glitzy jacket, a nerd may bring in eyeglasses or wear a nerdy hair style. These are small touches but make effective character statements. Best of all they don't require worries about damage, storage, loss/theft on your part.

### Awards/Videotapes and Other Culminations

Think about giving your performers a ribbon or small certificate, or a prize to indicate a job well done? Can you have a cast party?

And try to arrange for someone to video tape, or take pictures. Showing these to the performers makes a nice culmination.

## On Your Way

The whole experience should be fun. Exhausting but energizing. Unpredictable but set on firm ground. It should be an inspiration and enlightenment for teacher/leader and students alike. It should get students reading and memorizing and using critical thinking and social interaction skills without even knowing it! It should get teacher/leaders listening, communicating, interacting . . . educating students in new and exciting ways.

Enjoy!

꿈 꿈 꿈

## Bibliography

Rockwood, Jerome, *The Craftsmen of Dionysus,* Scott, Foresman and Company, Glenview, Illinois, 1966

Linklater, Kristin, *Freeing the Natural Voice,* Drama Book Publishers, New York, 1978

Eisenson, John *Voice and Diction,* Macmillan Publishing Company, New York, 1985

Stanislavski, Constantin, *An Actor Prepares,* Theatre Arts Books, New York, 1948

Spolin, Vola, *Improvisation for the Theatre,* Northwestern University Press, Evanston, Illinois, 1963

# YAAY ME!

This is a play designed to give every child a chance to publicly declare what it is that he/she is most proud of. The format remains the same, but the content changes with each performing group — because each child has something unique to say.

I originally created it when I had twenty students, with whom I met once a week for seven weeks. At the end of the session, I had to stage a piece, NO LONGER THAN TEN MINUTES, in which everyone had to have a speaking part! The objective, I decided, was to get every student to feel good about him or herself and that moment in the spotlight. I decided to create a piece celebrating each child's individual accomplishments.

I conducted a series of 2-minute interviews in which I asked each student: "Name one thing that you really do well, that makes you really feel proud of yourself." They all got a chance to hear each other's responses and I got real insight into each participant. The verses were easy once I knew the right kinds of things to write.

In creating your own version, you may want to lay out the verses written here and have the students select which one is most appropriate to them. You may want to give each student the assignment to write his/her own. Or you may want to conduct interviews to generate your own verses. I've included my questions, which you may find helpful in getting the students to talk about what they do. It's important to conduct these interviews in a non-judgemental, safe and trusting environment. Respect the answers and encourage students to respect their classmates' answers. I had a few students who said, "I don't have anything that I do well. I can't think of anything." How validating to then have people in the group say, "Yes you do. What about . . .?" The group members were able to articulate what was special and worthwhile about the person with low esteem.

I happen to be a fairly good note taker. If you'd rather put more attention on the live discussion, plan to audio tape it. You just want to get the raw material down. It may take you a few days to come up with a rhyming verse. You may choose to skip the rhyme and just come up with a mini- monologue.

Here are some questions I found useful:

- · What do you like most about this accomplishment?
- · How did you get started at it?
- · What does it feel like when you're doing it?
- · What do your family and friends think about it.

I had the entire cast onstage for the whole show. My goal for the opening was to get everyone on stage and give everyone a line. As each person did his/her verse, the rest of the cast did a pantomime of the activity. For example:

- · For the **baby sitter** I had other cast members seated around her, acting like little kids, sucking a thumb, twisting their hair, having a silent tantrum, pulling on the baby sitter's clothes, wrestling, etc.
- · For the **nature lover**, I had the entire cast act out plants or animals which she would then go around and water or pat.
- · The **writer** was seated center stage thinking and writing in his imaginary journal, while the rest of the cast made an action tableau of his fantasies behind him.

I've found this show to be a real team builder. Let the students find ways and make suggestions for how they can pantomime each person's verse.

Music — an "I'm terrific" self-validating kind of song —makes a rousing finale.

# YAAY ME!
## A Version for 16 Children

| | |
|---|---|
| **APRIL:** | Welcome one and all! |
| **TARA:** | Ladies and gentlemen |
| **ERIN:** | Parents and guardians |
| **GINA:** | Brothers and sisters |
| **HANNAH:** | Relatives and friends |
| **DAVID:** | Faculty and staff |
| **JADA:** | Young and old |
| **MATT:** | Beloved pets |
| **FAWN:** | Recent acquaintances |
| **LENNY:** | Stray members of tour groups |
| **CELINE:** | Animals, vegetables, minerals |
| **TOM:** | Creatures and extra-terrestials . . . |
| **PEGGY:** | Are you crazy? There aren't any E.T.'s out there. |
| **PHOEBE:** | We have to make sure to include everyone. |
| **YASSI:** | But the whole show is only ten minutes long. |
| **ALL:** | All right then, everybody, ready, set, go! |
| **TOM:** | There are times when I know I'm terrific, I'm proud |
| **PHOEBE:** | I want to shout "I AM THE GREATEST!" out loud. |
| **GINA:** | I'm here to tell you what's so great about me. |
| **PEGGY:** | Quite frankly, I'm marvelous as can be. |
| **CELINE:** | I'm sunny, I'm cute, a real pleasure to see |
| **ERIN:** | I have intelligence, wit and sensitivity. |
| **LENNY:** | There's quite often something unique that I did. |
| **MATT:** | And I say to myself, "Hey, you're all right, kid!" |
| **APRIL:** | We want you to share what we treasure inside |
| **HILARY:** | What *we* like about *us*, what we do with great pride. |
| **TOM:** | Acid drops, ollies and even hand plants<br>I leap and I swivel, I spin and I dance<br>Of one thing, I'm king, I am master and lord<br>I rule the whole world on my Pro- wing skate board. |
| **HANNAH:** | With pen and white paper, I'm better than best<br>I get A's on each one of my handwriting tests.<br>When it comes to old cursive, there's nobody better.<br>I put curliques, loops, even bows on each letter. |
| **ERIN:** | When the playground gets crazy, they call me if you please.<br>"Stop the fight, oh please help us!" — I put them at ease.<br>I'm the peace-maker, yes, I can stop any fight<br>Get both kids to shake hands and make everything right. |

16

| | |
|---|---|
| **PEGGY:** | My phone's always ringing, it jumps off the hook. |
| | I've got 31 Moms in my customer book. |
| | When it comes to child care, there's just nobody fitter |
| | I have fun, and I'm really a great baby sitter. |
| **LENNY:** | Wearing my chef hat and apron, BEWARE! |
| | Don't enter the kitchen when I'm working there. |
| | I can cook, yes I can, and my specialty is |
| | Marshmallow, grape jam and a touch of Cheez Whiz. |
| **ALL:** | YUCK! |
| **MATT:** | I help out my classmates in math and in reading |
| | I do well, but I never get into competing. |
| | I'm a number one student, I get A's take my word |
| | But I'm never a show off, I'm sure not a nerd. |
| **CELINE:** | I make friends very quickly, I'm not nervous or shy |
| | If I see someone new, I just smile and say, "Hi!" |
| | I have friends of all races, all cultures and hue |
| | My friends have all taught me so much that is new. |
| **PHOEBE:** | Please pick up that book, don't leave junk on my bed |
| | And please don't get ink on my sweater of red. |
| | I'm proud of my room, everything's super neat |
| | And I always dress cool, from my head to my feet. |
| **GINA:** | I am quite a performer, I'm great for my age |
| | I am proud of my dancing up here on the stage |
| | I rehearse and sometimes all my muscles get sore |
| | But I have so much fun when I get on the floor. |
| **HILARY:** | I'm studying Spanish, and I don't mean to boast |
| | But I say "Bien Venido!" when I'm playing host |
| | I take lessons each week and I can't even wait |
| | To say "Gracias!" for what I appreciate. |
| **FAWN:** | I am kind to all animals, I treat plants with care. |
| | As Mother Nature's helper, I do more than my share. |
| | Sick kittens grow well with my care and I bet |
| | When I grow up I'll make one heck of a vet. |
| **APRIL:** | I wear an orange belt on my shoulder up high. |
| | I'm always alert as the traffic goes by. |
| | I am crossing patrol at my school, with one arm |
| | I make sure kids cross safely and don't come to harm. |
| **JADA:** | I love classical concerts, I love a front seat. |
| | To see a great pianist is always a treat. |
| | I play piano and 'though I must practice for hours |
| | My recital was great and my Dad gave me flowers. |
| **DAVID:** | My imagination is sharp as can be |
| | I make up wild stories and write them with glee. |
| | My journal is special, I'm real good at writing |
| | My poems and stories are always exciting. |

| | |
|---|---|
| **TARA:** | When it comes to playing, stick around and you'll see<br>I'm creative with truck loads of energy.<br>My games and ideas are the best on the block<br>On weekends my friends and I play 'round the clock. |
| **YASSI:** | I stretch, I warm up, I lift my knees high.<br>I touch down to my toes, then reach up to the sky.<br>I go jogging each day and race once in awhile;<br>I won a red ribbon for a very fast mile. |
| **FAWN:** | So when I feel blue, dragging chin on the ground |
| **YASSI:** | A friend hurts my feelings, a teacher puts me down . . . |
| **JADA:** | If one of my parents gets angry, real mad |
| **TARA:** | When I do something silly or something real bad |
| **HANNAH:** | Or my brother and sister tease, laugh and make fun |
| **DAVID:** | Of something I've written, or spoken or done. |
| **ALL:** | When grey clouds pass over, I may cry awhile<br>But then I say this and I brighten my smile.<br>I can't always be perfect as perfect can be.<br>But I'm getting there, I try hard, I'm special<br>YAAY ME! |

## The End.

# A LUNCH LINE

## Introduction

I saw *A Chorus Line* (the play) four times and bought the album. I was intrigued by taking this show's format and setting it in a cafeteria lunch line. With this concept in mind you may wish to borrow lots of other stylistic and staging ideas.

I actually staged this in an all purpose room/cafeteria. I used masking tape for the lunch line, put down on a diagonal at the back of the room. I had portable dance mirrors act as the backstage wall. I used the piece "One" from *A Chorus Line* as each performer entered, holding a lunch tray up on front of his/her face. Each performer had taped a picture of him/herself to the bottom of the tray (a photocopied, enlarged version of his/her school picture). The only other props we used were school books, a skate board for David, and one chair.

The intros were written to reflect the personalities of each character.

This particular version has one scene and three monologues. For a larger cast, you may wish to borrow scenes and monologues from elsewhere in this book. Some suggestions:

- Rainbow Girls
- Beautiful
- Smart Dude
- Annie Matic
- No Justice
- Cool Breeze
- The Big A

The lunch line rap at the end (Jam/Jam) should be rhythmic, with lots of snapping, clapping and dancing. You can certainly substitute your school's football or basketball cheer here.

## Cast

**Missy**

**Kathy**

**Andy**

**Sarah**

**Tory**

**David**

# A LUNCH LINE

*The cast is onstage, lined up in the lunch line. Each actor has a lunch tray with his/her picture taped to the back. Each holds the tray up in front of her face. One by one they introduce themselves.*

**MISSY:** Hi. I'm Missy. Wait. Hello, my name is Missy. No . . . Good evening. How do you do. My name is Missy.

**ANDY:** Look, I don't know how long I'll be here. Anyway, my name is Andy. Everything else is on my school records. They should be here any day now.

**TORY:** I'm Victoria. My friends call me Tory. But my stage name will be Samantha Swann. Isn't it great? Don't I look like I could be a Samantha Swann?

**SARAH:** The Formula. Step 1. Hi, I'm Sarah. I'm really glad to meet you. So where are you from? What are your hobbies?

**KATHY:** Hi. I'm Kathy. I get the best grades. The teachers like me. I really like Todd Chapman. And I am not a nerd.

**DAVID:** How's it going? It's a veritable condominium of marine life. Bilingual aviators are virtually furious. I'm David.

**ALL:** The lunch line. It's a place to get hot, body- building nourishment to sustain us through the school day.

**ANDY:** Yech. What is that? Mystery meat?

**MISSY:** Bologna from home is better than that.

**TORY:** God, it looks like worms.

**SARAH:** Disgusting. My dog wouldn't eat that.

**DAVID:** I saw that serving guy spit in it.

**ALL:** Gross out. Barf. Gag me with a spoon.

**ANDY:** It's a place for friendly camaraderie.

**SARAH:** Hey, you butt in.

**ANDY:** I was here before.

**MISSY:** Don't push me.

**SARAH:** I said move.

**ANDY:** Get off me.

*The rest of the kids break it up.*

**ALL:** It's where we make friends and build school spirit.

**TORY:** Will you look at what she's wearing?

**MISSY:** I hate her.

**SARAH:** She looks so stupid.

**MISSY:** And she thinks she's so cool!

**ALL:** Where young love blossoms.

**KATHY:** You never take me to parties.

**DAVID:** I hate parties.

| | |
|---|---|
| **MISSY:** | All you care about is that crappy old skate board. |
| **DAVID:** | Don't you call my skate board crappy. |
| **MISSY:** | You're crappy. |
| **DAVID:** | You're history. |
| **ALL:** | It's a place where we can discuss school work with our classmates. |
| **KATHY:** | Missy! Missy! Hey, Missy. So when do you want to meet? |
| **MISSY:** | I don't have time to talk now. I'll see you later. |
| **KATHY:** | Well, I'm leaving school early. I thought we should set up a time. |
| **MISSY:** | I can't talk now. |
| **KATHY:** | Because we need to get started. We've got a lot of work to cover. |
| **MISSY:** | Listen, I don't know, O.K.? |
| **KATHY:** | What about Monday? |
| **MISSY:** | I have ballet. |
| **KATHY:** | Tuesday? |
| **MISSY:** | Cheerleaders. |
| **KATHY:** | I'm free Thursday. |
| **MISSY:** | I'm not. |
| **KATHY:** | It's Friday then? |
| **MISSY:** | No. I'm having a party Friday night. |
| **KATHY:** | You are? |
| **MISSY:** | Yeah. For some of my friends. |
| | *Pause.* |
| **KATHY:** | So do you want to start with some of the easy equations? |
| **MISSY:** | Would you keep your voice down? |
| **KATHY:** | What do you want to work on first? |
| **MISSY:** | I don't care. |
| **KATHY:** | What do you have problems with? |
| **MISSY:** | What are you, a shrink? I don't have any problems. |
| **KATHY:** | So why did you ask Mrs. Maggio for a tutor? |
| **MISSY:** | She told me to get one. |
| **KATHY:** | She said you asked her first. |
| **MISSY:** | What else did she tell you? |
| **KATHY:** | It's nothing to be ashamed of. |
| **MISSY:** | Well I don't want you broadcasting it, understand? You want me to broadcast your problems? Oh, I guess you don't have any. Wonder Girl over here gets it all right. |
| **KATHY:** | No. Math's just my best subject. |
| **MISSY:** | Everything's your best subject. A in Math, A in History. A in Biology. |

| | |
|---|---|
| **KATHY:** | I study. |
| **MISSY:** | You've got plenty of time. I guess you've got nothing else to do. |
| **KATHY:** | I babysit. |
| **MISSY:** | (*Sarcastically*) Whoa! |
| **KATHY:** | I'm in the chess club. |
| **MISSY:** | (*Sarcastically*) Major excitement! |

*Pause.*

| | |
|---|---|
| **KATHY:** | We could meet at my house. My Mom makes these fabulous Rocky Road cookies. |
| **MISSY:** | Listen, read my lips, O.K.? I don't want to meet at your house. I don't want your mother's Rocky Road cookies. I want you to leave me alone. |

*KATHY walks away. MISSY runs after her.*

| | |
|---|---|
| | Wait! Wait a minute. Damn, how did I get into this mess? |
| **KATHY:** | You asked Maggio. If you changed your mind, that's O.K. |
| **MISSY:** | I don't want to go to your house. |
| **KATHY:** | That's O.K. I'll come to your house. |
| **MISSY:** | That's completely out of the question. We'll meet in the library at 8:00 on Saturday morning. |
| **KATHY:** | Nobody goes to the library at 8:00 on Saturday. |
| **MISSY:** | Exactly. You're catching on. Now listen, you come in the Kelly Street door. I'll enter about 10 minutes later by Rockland Court. You find a table in the back of the reading room. Walk straight back and don't draw attention to yourself. |
| **KATHY:** | What? |
| **MISSY:** | I'll come in after you. Don't call out or wave. I'll find you. |
| **KATHY:** | I don't understand. |
| **MISSY:** | You're supposed to be smart. |
| **KATHY:** | I don't see why I can't come to your house. |
| **MISSY:** | Because we don't want the whole world to know, O.K.? Get it? Saturday at 8 for a few hours and that's it. |
| **KATHY:** | You know, you act as if you're doing me a favor. |
| **MISSY:** | I am. |
| **KATHY:** | By getting me up at 8 on my one day to sleep late? By allowing me to teach you math? By making me cram a year's worth of work into a Saturday morning only because you were dumb enough to skip all those math classes. Tell me again, how is this a favor to me? |
| **MISSY:** | I know what you're doing. You approach me in the middle of all my friends. People you wouldn't dare approach any other time. You're just using me to get in. |
| **KATHY:** | In what? |

| | |
|---|---|
| **MISSY:** | In my group. |
| **KATHY:** | I don't want to be in your group. |
| **MISSY:** | Come on. It's embarrassing. You're always trying to force yourself on us. You walk into the middle of a conversation, trying to laugh and joke when you don't even know what we're talking about. You shouldn't be so pushy. You can't expect to fit in just like that. |
| **KATHY:** | Who says I want to fit in? |
| **MISSY:** | You figure here's your big break. Maggio says you tutor me in math and you think you're in. |
| **KATHY:** | I don't want to be in. I have my own friends. |
| **MISSY:** | Oh, right, the nerd herd. Listen, I've got nothing against you personally, but you're going about this all wrong. Give it time. Maybe by next year people will be used to you. |
| **KATHY:** | I haven't got time. |
| **MISSY:** | Well, it doesn't happen overnight. You can't go where you don't belong. |
| **KATHY:** | How do you know where I belong? |
| **MISSY:** | Come on. I mean I don't want to hurt your feelings, but look at the way you dress. I mean, nothing personal. But it's too weird. People laugh at you. |
| **KATHY:** | So what? |
| **MISSY:** | If you don't care then you're worse off than I thought. |
| **KATHY:** | Yeah, well, I gotta go. |
| | *She walks away.* |
| **MISSY:** | Wait. Wait a minute. You asked me to tell you the truth. That's the truth. |
| **KATHY:** | You know what I think? I think you're scared. You're so scared somebody's going to take away your power. You're afraid somebody's going to be better than you . . . at anything. So you always have to put everybody else down. You always have to be the prettiest, the most popular, the coolest. |
| **MISSY:** | I can't help that. |
| **KATHY:** | (*Shouting.*) Only it's hard to be cool when you're flunking everything. |
| **MISSY:** | Shut up! |
| **KATHY:** | It's your life. |
| **MISSY:** | Wait. Wait. |
| **KATHY:** | What? |
| **MISSY:** | Will you stop walking away like that. You're pissing me off. |
| **KATHY:** | I thought we were finished. |
| **MISSY:** | So it's Saturday morning at the library. |
| **KATHY:** | You're crazy. |
| **MISSY:** | You come in the Kelly Street door. |
| | *Pause.* |
| **KATHY:** | Why do you want a tutor? What are you doing this for? |

| | |
|---|---|
| **MISSY:** | What do you mean, I'm flunking math. |
| **KATHY:** | So, what do you care? You and your friends party all the time anyway. You've got your 36-22-36 figure and your pink Lauren sundresses. What do you care if you're flunking math? |
| **MISSY:** | It's my parents. I don't want to disappoint them. |
| **KATHY:** | Bull. They give you anything you want. If you didn't like the school, they'd buy you a brand new one. So what's the deal? |
| **MISSY:** | None of your business. |
| **KATHY:** | What's the deal or I broadcast that you asked Maggio for a tutor? |
| | *Pause.* |
| **MISSY:** | They want me to do ninth grade again. |
| **KATHY:** | Oh. I get it. And then you'd have to fit in. All over again. |
| **MISSY:** | If you say anything to absolutely anyone, I swear I'll make you sorry. |
| **KATHY:** | Gee, you're in a tough spot. I'd like to help you but I can't. |
| **MISSY:** | What! |
| **KATHY:** | I just remembered, I've got an appointment on Saturday morning. |
| **MISSY:** | Well then in the afternoon. |
| **KATHY:** | I'm busy then too. |
| **MISSY:** | Well, I can't do it any other day. |
| **KATHY:** | As a matter of fact, I really think my work load's too heavy for me to tutor you at all. |
| **MISSY:** | What? |
| **KATHY:** | Find someone else. |
| **MISSY:** | You're kidding, right? |
| **KATHY:** | Nope. |
| | *Walks away.* |
| **MISSY:** | (*Pulling her.*) Cut it out! Come back here. |
| **KATHY:** | What is it now? |
| **MISSY:** | You have to do it. |
| **KATHY:** | (*Laughing.*) I do not. |
| **MISSY:** | Maggio told you to. |
| **KATHY:** | Wrong, she asked me to. She likes me. |
| **MISSY:** | Look, we'll get together at your house Saturday afternoon. |
| **KATHY:** | Nope. |
| **MISSY:** | My house? |
| **KATHY:** | Getting warmer. |
| **MISSY:** | We'll start with the easy equations. |
| **KATHY:** | Gee, I don't know. . . |

| MISSY: | Come on. |
|---|---|
| KATHY: | What's in it for me? |
| MISSY: | What do you mean? I'm not paying you, that's for sure. |
| KATHY: | I don't want money. |
| MISSY: | What do you want then? |

*Pause.*

| KATHY: | Sarah, Terry and me at your party — Friday night. |
|---|---|
| MISSY: | What? |
| KATHY: | Or no equations. |
| MISSY: | Now wait, you don't understand. I've already invited all the people. |
| KATHY: | Now there's three more. |
| MISSY: | Three extra girls? That's too many. |
| KATHY: | I wonder how many girls will be in your class next year, if you repeat ninth grade. |
| MISSY: | This is blackmail. |
| KATHY: | Yup. |
| MISSY: | I trusted you with a very important secret. |
| KATHY: | Do we get invited? |

*Pause.*

| MISSY: | O.K., you can come. But promise me, if you're not asked to dance, and you definitely won't be, please don't start dancing with each other! |
|---|---|
| KATHY: | What time? |
| MISSY: | Eleven. Now it's just you three. Don't bring anyone else. |
| KATHY: | Just us. Who's going to be there? |
| MISSY: | Nobody you know. |
| KATHY: | Todd Chapman? |
| MISSY: | You don't know Todd. You don't hang out with any of these people. They hardly know you exist. You're going to have a miserable time. |
| KATHY: | Don't worry about it. |
| MISSY: | You won't fit in. |
| KATHY: | If you're having a party, I'm coming. It beats a Wheel of Fortune re-run. Even if I sit all night just talking to Sarah and Terry, it'll still be worth it. I'm going to get a kick out of seeing you explain why we're invited. |
| MISSY: | You swore you wouldn't tell. |
| KATHY: | I didn't swear, but I won't tell. That's eleven o'clock Friday night. And I'll be sure to bring along some of those Rocky Road cookies. |
| MISSY: | Oh God! |

æ  æ  æ

**TORY:** The lunch line is the place to meet your buddies. Where you hang out with your own special group of friends. The lunch line can te a terrible place when you're the new kid.

**ANDY:** Every morning I check the mirror to make sure I haven't grown old overnight. It could happen. Today's vibrant adolescent is tomorrow's old bag. Of course I think about growing old. MY life is speeding by so fast I feel like I'm chasing it, not in it. They say if you're in a car wreck, your whole life passes before you. I couldn't even see mine — ZOOOOOM. Gone. I've been to six different schools in six different states in six years. When I was little and they called attendance, I thought "Transfer" was my last name. It's Dad's job that's got us nuts. Today Minneapolis, tomorrow Cheyenne, next week Des Moines. Earth to Dad! Earth to Dad! Come in Dad! My mother won't even plant real flowers anymore. She just screws in the big plastic azalea bushes in front of each house, then rips them out again when we move. I'm embarrassed for my life. My brother's only three and keeps his toys in a trunk. He's afraid to take them out to play because the movers might forget them. My family is a collection of weirdos. Me? I've got a vision of wearing roller skates to my senior prom. Somewhere in Mule City, North Dakota. Tied to the fender of the car, so Dad can pull me past the gym on prom night, as we speed on to the next town. Zoom. Listen, I could make friends if we stayed in one place longer than a minute.

🙊 🙊 🙊

**DAVID:** But some kids have the knack. They could fit in any place.

**SARAH:** I finally got tired of being the "New Girl." I was killing myself trying to make friends and break into groups that had cemented long before I got there. I said to myself, "There's gotta be a better way to get through life. I gotta come up with a formula." We were stationed in South Carolina at the time. I was Sarah. Not Mary Jane or Sally May. Just Sarah, "The New Girl." The only natural blond. I wore braces and I had a Yankee accent. The formula hit me in the middle of crying myself to sleep for the fifth night in a row. I said to myself, "Wait a minute. Everybody's got the same set of buttons, you just gotta be smart enough to know which ones to push." I developed a kind of universal code — a generic brand personality that works like a charm. I'm nice enough to the boys so they won't think I'm snotty, but not so nice that I piss off the girls. I'm nice enough to the nerds, 'cause I never know when I'll have to copy on a test. But I don't hang out with them, because then I'd be one too, see? I'm nice to the teachers, but I never smile or let them think I'm really learning anything. I never compete with the most popular girl and I make sure to dress two steps below her. I never trust any girl with a secret. I never get into any boy's car alone. And I never let anybody see me cry. It works. This way, I slip in and out of schools all the time, without any crap. And on days when I get the urge to set a lab on fire or spray paint the flag pole, or put my fist through a classroom window, I just go home and scream into my pillow, blasting Def Leppard through the earphones directly into my brain. And then, I'm just fine.

26

**TORY:** And then there's the loner. He doesn't have to fit in. He's a group in himself.

**DAVID:** I was skating around about eleven p.m. I picked up the purr of a BMW over my left shoulder. They were closing in fast and I was about a mile from home. They honked. "Hey you! Hey you *BLEEP,* what do you think you're doin' man?" I sped on. If I stopped, if I answered, I was dead meat. "Hey you *BLEEP*, I'm talking to you *BLEEP BLEEP!*" Any minute I expected the screech of brakes. Then two large middle class boys would leap from the sedan and beat the hell out of me for no reason at all. Luckily, I was bearing down fast on Selkirk and they had to get out of the turn lane where a car was stalled. I swiveled right onto Selkirk and lost them. I'm a skate rat. Lots of people ride skate boards, but they're not skate rats.

*Shows off his skateboard.*

See how ripped up and battered this is. I got this when I almost busted my butt on a curb. Some guys will take screwdrivers and gouge up a $150 board they never even rode, just for the effect. I got my board the old-fashioned way. I earned it. Skate rats hate car rats. Car rats hate skate rats. Mall rats hate skate rats too. You know you're a mall rat if you dress exactly like your friends, wear too much make up, spend all day at the mall without buying anything, and talk like this, "Oh my God, oh my God, oh my God. I mean skate rats are so un-cool, I mean, they're just un-cool." I'm a skate rat. I've been put in detention for defying the ban and riding to class. I've been grounded by my Dad, hounded by car rats and ridiculed by mall rats. Even the pretty ones. But I'm a skate rat. I'll meet the challenge. The rest of them can kiss my *BLEEP.*

ia ia ia

**ANDY:** Most of all, we want to be O.K. Most of all we just want to be given a chance and respected for taking a risk. That's what makes it so hard when we get shot down.

**TORY:** I saw *A Chorus Line* eight times. That's why I signed up for the drama club. God, it's the greatest show in the entire world.

*Sings.*

"One! Singular sensation every little step she takes. . ." I only want to play Morales. So I'm red-headed and Jewish. I could play a Puerto Rican.

*Sings.*

"Who am I, anyway, am I my resume?" I could play the hell out of Morales. Remember her from acting class?

*She sings a few lines from the show.*

27

I love that. I mean I can really feel what she felt. I had a teacher like Karp who humiliated me through an entire summer school English class. I can't wait until she opens up a *People* magazine and discovers that the same Tory Kraus she degraded and ridiculed is now the famous Samantha Swann. Hah! Eat your heart out!

❧　❧　❧

**KATHY:** You're in charge. You make the rules. No talking. No running. No skateboards in the hall. No jamming in the lunch line. No jamming. Jam. Jam. Jam. Jam.

**ALL:** Jam/Jam/A Jibba/A Jam/Jibba Jibba/Jam Jam/Jam on.

*Repeat.*

**SARAH:**
We want what's cool
We want what's in
We want to be what's happenin'

**KATHY:**
We might try smoke
We might try drink
But we're not as dumb as you might think.

**DAVID:**
Clothes and money, sex and cars
Kids walk around like movie stars.

**MISSY:**
It's all out here for a song.
It's hard to know what's right from wrong.

**ANDY:**
We've got decisions, plans to make
And sometimes it's too much to take.

**ALL:** Jam/Jam/A Jibba/A Jam/Jibba Jibba/Jam Jam/Jam on.

*Repeat.*

**TORY:**
We drive our parents round the bend
But we're catchin' hell here on our end.

**ANDY:**
We'll play it safe but we won't hide
Cause we've got time on our side.

**MISSY:**
We've got to march to our own drum
In the pie of life we've got the plum.

**ALL:** JAM ON!

**ANDY:** If we seem scared —

**KATHY:** Or look confused,

**SARAH:** Just don't forget —

**DAVID:** We're payin' dues.

**MISSY:** Love us, trust us —

| | |
|---|---|
| **TORY:** | That's the key — |
| **ALL:** | To let us be what we want to be. |

ЄⱭ  ЄⱭ  ЄⱭ

| | |
|---|---|
| **SARAH:** | The Lunch Line. It probably looks the same in any school, on any day, anywhere in the world. Kids lined up waiting for hot lunch. Lined up ready and waiting to become what they dream of. |
| **MISSY:** | I want to be like Bette Midler. Not the really outrageous stuff. But she doesn't care what people think of her. I want to walk into the cafeteria one day, take a deep breath and shout: "I'm Missy. I'm my own person. To hell with ballet and cheerleaders and the dance committee. I'm my own person." I'd stand on my own. And I wouldn't have to give parties just to know I could get friends. |
| **ANDY:** | I'm Andy and I'm here. I don't know for how long, but I'm going to make the best of what I've got. I waste a lot of time trying to hold on to time I don't have. Maybe a five month friend is O.K. Maybe that's all I need right now. At least I'd have that. I want to be like Ally Sheedy. Versatile, adaptable, likeable. |
| **DAVID:** | So I guess you're expecting me to admit that I want to be a car rat or a mall rat. Not me. I'm O.K. just the way I am. When I dream of what I want to be, I see me just as I am now. I'm just fine. (*Pause.*) Only . . . I wouldn't mind . . . you know . . . finding a girl who thinks I'm just fine too. |
| **KATHY:** | I'm not giving up my soul for Todd Chapman either. I'm still Kathy, and I'm not playing dumb just to be cool. Remember in St. Elmo's Fire, Wendy, the really quiet one, got Rob Lowe in the end. That's not bad. |
| **TORY:** | I'm Tory, alias Samantha Swann. I want glitz and excitement. I will not be an ordinary person, and I refuse to live an ordinary life. So maybe Samantha Swann's too much. Maybe I'll change. But I won't give up my dreams. Never. How about Maria Montclair? Nice? |
| **SARAH:** | I'm Sarah and I don't want to be anyone special. I just want to be O.K. That doesn't sound like much. But I know if keep up this act, if I keep getting by on the formula, I'm bound to blow. Pow! And then everybody will see what's really been inside all along. And, hey, I just want to be O.K. |

*Hot Lunch Jam swells to a crescendo, actors hold the trays up in front of their faces.*

# DO YOU LIKE ME?
## Written for Black Kids in Theatre

## March, 1988

## Introduction

Adolescents are intensely concerned about making friends and being popular. They sometimes find themselves going to great lengths, even getting into trouble, to keep friends, stay with the in-group and command respect.

In order to develop this piece, I asked students to think about the things people do to get others to like them. The discussion started off with fairly obvious things we do: act friendly, honestly, courteously. As the group warmed up a little more, we got into how we sometimes go to extremes to gain popularity: showing off, complimenting people excessively, talking too much, throwing money around. Based on our discussion, I created *Do You Like Me?* I use this phrase throughout the play, because it seems to be the burning question among adolescents, and among a heck of a lot of adults as well!

For the opening, I had a tableau, with each performer in a physical pose appropriate to his/her character. The only props and costumes we used were in the second scene (play money and a jacket). I did not use music, sets, or lights.

The monologues were done straight to the audience. Some of the characters (Tanya) were stationary, while others (Anna and Sarah) moved non-stop. In all the scenes, we used stop action and freeze, in order to allow the characters to come out of the action and speak directly to the audience.

The ending was a reprise, with characters speaking directly to the audience, with all the intensity and desperation they could muster.

## Cast

| | |
|---|---|
| **Sammy** | **Felicity** |
| **Mary** | **Anna** |
| **Bobby** | **Marvin** |
| **Chris** | **Sarah** |
| **Betty** | **Tanya** |
| | **Millie** |

| | |
|---|---|
| **SAMMY:** | I'll do what you tell me<br>I'll follow your rules<br>I follow the guy<br>Who's the bully in school<br>Do you like me? |
| **MARY:** | My Mom lets me wear lipstick<br>Wear high heels and pantyhose<br>I go to all the fancy adult places<br>That she often goes<br>Do you like me? |
| **BOBBY:** | I'm strong, just feel my muscles<br>I'm really rough and tough<br>I can hold you down and make you scream<br>Until you shout "ENOUGH!"<br>Do you like me? |
| **CHRIS:** | I'm the classroom clown and baby<br>I keep everyone enthused<br>My jokes come one per second<br>I keep all my friends amused.<br>Do you like me? |
| **BETTY:** | I'm always complimentary<br>I treat everybody well<br>I hide what I might really think<br>So you can never tell.<br>Do you like me? |
| **FELICITY:** | I make up little stories<br>I wouldn't call them lies<br>They just make me more interesting<br>And keep my friends surprised.<br>Do you like me? |
| **ANNA:** | I am a marvelous actress<br>Onstage a dozen times or more<br>And when I dance I'm fabulous<br>The queen of the dance floor.<br>Do you like me? |
| **MARVIN:** | I've got tons of money<br>I bring lots to school each day<br>Even kids who hate my guts<br>Become friends, 'cause I pay<br>Do you like me? |
| **SARAH:** | I'm studious, hardworking<br>I get A's on every test<br>I'm teacher's pet, but that's because<br>I am the very best<br>Do you like me? |

| TANYA: | When it comes to conversation |
| | I'm smart, I'm bright, I'm quick |
| | My tongue can run, no-pause, non-stop |
| | On any subject that you pick. |
| | Do you like me? |
| MILLIE: | I'm so very meek and quiet |
| | You won't even know I'm here |
| | I want to say what's on my mind |
| | But I'm too full of fear |
| | Do you like me? |
| ALL: | We've told you who we are |
| | So we can't run and hide |
| | But what we'll show you now |
| | Is what we really feel inside! |

ða ða ða

**BETTY:** Sometimes I feel like a wind-up doll. Watch me go. "Hi, that's a lovely sweater. Hi, you wanna sleep over tonight? Hi, you look terrific today. Hi, oooh I wish my hair was like yours." Sometimes I amaze myself with the things I come up with. Give me the lowest, slimiest, sleeziest creep and I bet you I could come up with a compliment. I once even complimented a girl on her braces! "Nice retainer and those rubber bands are so cute." Dumb! I know. But it's quick. It's the easy way to move in and out of these groups. I'm never alone. Everyone's a sucker for a compliment. So they like having me around. You know the funny thing? Nobody ever gives me a compliment. Gee, I wish someone would find something nice to say about me. And really mean it. Could you think of something? Do you like me?

ða ða ða

## Scene One

| MARY: | He's just so adorable. |
| FELICITY: | Oh I know. He's soooo cute. |
| MARY: | I'm going to marry him. |
| MILLIE: | You're only 12. Aren't you rushing things? |
| MARY: | Did you say something? |
| MILLIE: | No. |
| FELICITY: | I think he's so cool when he wears that denim jacket. |
| MARY: | With the collar turned up. |
| FELICITY: | Ooooh. |

| | |
|---|---|
| **MILLIE:** | He should wear his snow jacket in this weather. |
| **FELICITY:** | Did you say something? |
| **MILLIE:** | Forget it. |
| **FELICITY:** | He called me last week. |
| **MILLIE:** | He did? |
| **MARY:** | He didn't! |
| **FELICITY:** | He did! |
| **MARY:** | When? |
| **FELICITY:** | Friday night. |
| **MILLIE:** | You spent the night at my house Friday night. |
| **FELICITY:** | Then it must have been Thursday night. I got mixed up. |
| **MILLIE:** | You never mentioned it to me. |
| **FELICITY:** | He actually invited me for pizza. But my Mom said I couldn't go. |
| **MILLIE:** | Felicity? |
| **FELICITY:** | He did! He did! I swear. And I think you're mean not to believe me. |
| **MILLIE:** | Well you know you can exaggerate every now and then. |
| **MARY:** | Now and then? This girl's a lie a minute. |
| **MILLIE:** | Mary, don't |
| **FELICITY:** | You're supposed to be my friend. |
| **MILLIE:** | They're more fibs than lies. |
| **MARY:** | Eddie Murphy is her uncle. Her father's a brain surgeon. She took spring break on the Riviera. You call those fibs? |
| **FELICITY:** | That's not true. I do not fib. |
| **MARY:** | There's another one! You tell us big stories and then you get in trouble when the truth comes out. |
| **MILLIE:** | I don't think we should talk about it. |
| **MARY:** | Millie, when you get more mature you'll realize that it's better to talk about these little problems. I know this because lots of my mother's friends are psychologists and geologists. |
| **MILLIE:** | Geologists study dirt. |
| **MARY:** | Whatever. Now Felicity, tell us the truth. Did he call you? |
| **FELICITY:** | Yes! |
| **MILLIE:** | And you spoke to him? |
| **FELICITY:** | Yes! Yes! |
| **MARY:** | And he invited you out to pizza? |
| **FELICITY:** | I said yes. We had pizza then went to the movies and he held my hand and brought me home and walked me to my door and kissed me. On the lips! |
| **MARY:** | But you told us your Mom wouldn't let you go out with him. |
| **FELICITY:** | That was another time. |

| | |
|---|---|
| **MILLIE:** | Leave her alone, Mary. I hope you had a good time Felicity. I think you're really lucky. |
| **MARY:** | I think he's really lucky too. And I'm going to call him and tell him so. |
| **FELICITY:** | What? You wouldn't. You don't have his number. |
| **MARY:** | I have the school directory. |
| **FELICITY:** | Don't! |
| **MARY:** | Why not? |
| **FELICITY:** | His mother's sick. You'll disturb her. |
| **MILLIE:** | Mary, don't. |
| **MARY:** | If his mother's sick, he'll probably answer the phone. |
| **FELICITY:** | Don't! |
| **MARY:** | Why not? Why not, Felicity? Because it didn't happen? Because it's all a big fat lie? |
| **FELICITY:** | No! Yes! No! Ooooh, I hate you Millie. I'll never forgive you for this. |

*MARY and MILLIE freeze.*

**FELICITY:**
> I don't know why I do it.
> I don't know why, I swear
> I open my mouth to speak
> And the lie's just waiting there.
>
> If I always told the truth
> I'd be so ordinary
> And I'd lose all my friends.
> Including Millie and Mary.
> Would you like me?

*FELICITY runs out.*

| | |
|---|---|
| **MILLIE:** | How did she end up mad at me? I didn't do anything. |
| **MARY:** | It's common among children. I'm too strong for her to face. So she blames you. She'll get over it. |
| **MILLIE:** | You sure know a lot. |
| **MARY:** | If you weren't such a meek little mouse, if you got out and hung around with more sophisticated people, you wouldn't be so naive. Of course, I'm mature for my age. That's why he has such a crush on me. |
| **MILLIE:** | He does? |
| **MARY:** | He asked *me* out for pizza. |
| **MILLIE:** | Really? |
| **MARY:** | Last Saturday night. But I couldn't go. I never miss one of Mom's cocktail parties. |
| **MILLIE:** | You drink cocktails? |
| **MARY:** | No dummy. I drink 7 Up from a wine glass. I look so cool. |
| **MILLIE:** | Well, I'm sure glad you turned him down. |

| | |
|---|---|
| **MARY:** | Why? |
| **MILLIE:** | Because he called me. |
| **MARY:** | What? |
| **MILLIE:** | He called me and I went out with him. |
| **MARY:** | (*Laughing.*) Careful you don't catch Felicity's disease. |
| **MILLIE:** | We had pizza and drank 7 Up from paper cups. |
| **MARY:** | Well suppose I just call him to see if you're telling the truth. |
| **MILLIE:** | 724-3091. That's his number. I had to call him to say thanks. |
| **MARY:** | You're serious. You really did go out with him . . . on a DATE! |

*MARY freezes.*

**MILLIE:**

        I swore I wouldn't tell a soul
        He made me cross my heart
        But they think I'm meek and nerdy
        The news was bursting me apart.

        Sure I'm pretty quiet
        I'm often really shy
        But inside there's a wonderful girl
        Who wants to jump out and say "Hi!"
        Would you like me?

| | |
|---|---|
| **MARY:** | Well I just can't believe that he'd go out with someone like you. |
| **MILLIE:** | Like me how? |
| **MARY:** | Childish, immature, unsophisticated, meek, wimpish. |
| **MILLIE:** | Well, I'm not exciting like Felicity. I'm not sophisticated like you. But maybe, just maybe I'm fun to be with. Maybe he doesn't want lies or lectures. He just wants to relax and have fun with someone like me. Come on, walk me to the soda machine. We can drink 7 Up. From a can! |

*MILLIE freezes.*

**MARY:**

        I just can't believe it
        I'm on the verge of tears
        I can't believe he preferred her
        I can't believe my ears.

        I try to be mature
        Go to opera and restaurants
        But deep inside I'm still a child
        Who wants what every young girl wants.
        Would you like me?

                 ᔐ   ᔐ   ᔐ

**TANYA:** Detention again. They'll call my Mom and I'll get the same lecture. "Tanya you have to start paying attention in class. You have to learn to STOP TALKING!" Yeah, yeah, yeah. I've heard that all my life. But I can't help it. School is so boring. I talk to pass the time. To amuse myself. To amuse everyone. That's why I'm so popular. Oh, I am. I'm a walking, one-woman social whirl! There's no trick to it. I'm a born talker. I just hate the silence. It's so lonely. (*Pause.*) People say I'm going to be a lawyer or a politician. That's O.K. But I keep thinking that maybe one day I'll change. I'll grow up and settle down and be one of those sweet, quiet, soft-spoken women who listens but never speaks. Meek. Well-mannered. Can you picture that? Would you like me?

ಶಿ ಶಿ ಶಿ

**ANNA:** (*Very dramatically.*) Oh, I can't. I can't possibly get up here in front of all those people! Don't make me do it. Please! (*Abruptly.*) Hello. Did I fool you? Did you really think I was frightened? I'm an actress. Actually I think I'm going to be a very famous actress. I can do so many moods!

*She makes the appropriate poses.*

Pensive. Aggressive. Happy. Depressed. Desperate. Sly. Good huh? Actually, I'll tell you a secret . . . I'm so good sometimes, I don't know if I'm acting or it's for real. I guess it doesn't matter as long as I get what I want. Friends. Fame. Money. Power. Remember you saw me here first! I shouldn't be worried, should I? I shouldn't have to decide who I really want to be just yet, should I? I mean what if I chose the me that nobody liked? Would you like me?

ಶಿ ಶಿ ಶಿ

## Scene Two

**MARVIN:** Do you think $20 is enough?

**CHRIS:** Holy uba scuba, where did you get $20?

**MARVIN:** I've got lots more in my piggy bank. Not to mention stocks and bonds. Here, have a fiver.

**CHRIS:** Say, thanks!

**MARVIN:** I've got plenty of money. That's not my problem.

**CHRIS:** What could be a problem with all that money?

**MARVIN:** Bobby. He's on my case.

**CHRIS:** I'm outta here!

**MARVIN:** How'd you like ten bucks.

**CHRIS:** Does a polar bear sneeze icicles?

36

| | |
|---|---|
| **MARVIN:** | It's yours if you help me deal with Bobby. |
| **CHRIS:** | For ten bucks? |
| **MARVIN:** | For twenty? |
| **CHRIS:** | Bobby's gonna eat your toe nails off for lunch. Then he'll use my ears for cuff links. |
| **MARVIN:** | Thirty bucks for just standing here. |
| **CHRIS:** | Just standing here? |
| **MARVIN:** | And maybe saying something funny. You're good at that. Maybe he'll laugh the whole thing off . . . |
| **CHRIS:** | Nah! |
| **MARVIN:** | So will you just stand here? I figure you can be my witness if he murders me. |
| **CHRIS:** | Do you have a plan? |
| **MARVIN:** | What else? I'll offer him money. |
| **CHRIS:** | He'll take the money first, then kick your butt. |
| **MARVIN:** | Oh Chris. What am I going to do? |
| **CHRIS:** | Think fast, 'cause here comes Bobby! |

*BOBBY and SAMMY enter.*

| | |
|---|---|
| **SAMMY:** | So you want me to do your math and science dittos. Anything else? |
| **BOBBY:** | What do you think, slug brain? |
| **SAMMY:** | Spelling and language too? |
| **BOBBY:** | And try to make it sloppier. The teachers get suspicious if my work looks too neat. |
| **SAMMY:** | Right, Bobby. Anything else? |
| **BOBBY:** | Make sure Craig forks over that green pen. I like it. I want it. Just give him the message. He'll give up the pen. |
| **SAMMY:** | Right, Bobby. Anything you say. |
| **BOBBY:** | And stick around. This ought to be a laugh. (*To CHRIS.*) Hey, yo! |
| **CHRIS:** | Hey who? |
| **BOBBY:** | You! Don't play with me, clown! |
| **CHRIS:** | Now, you know I wouldn't do that, Bobby. I'm just takin' my usual recess stroll. (*Takes a deep breath.*) Ah, just smell that fresh gravel. Just look at the bloom on those monkey bars. Just strollin' along, minding my business. |
| **BOBBY:** | This clown is dumb. |
| **SAMMY:** | Dumb. |
| **BOBBY:** | But funny. |
| **SAMMY:** | Right, funny. |
| **BOBBY:** | And who are you, boy? |
| **MARVIN:** | Ten bucks, sir. |
| **BOBBY:** | That your name? |

| | |
|---|---|
| **MARVIN:** | Ten bucks if you let me go, sir. |
| **BOBBY:** | You believe this? |
| **SAMMY:** | Unbelievable! |
| **BOBBY:** | Who are you? |
| **MARVIN:** | Remember me? I'm Marvin. You said you were going to turn me into Marshmallow. But I've got twenty five bucks if you should happen to change your mind. |
| **CHRIS:** | Hey, Bobby, what a deal. Twenty five smackeroos! |
| **BOBBY:** | Shut up, Clown. |
| **SAMMY:** | Shut up! |
| **BOBBY:** | (*To MARVIN.*) As for you, weasel boy, I'm not going to turn you into marshmallow. |
| **MARVIN:** | Thank heavens. |
| **BOBBY:** | You're gonna look more like yogurt by the time I'm finished. |
| **SAMMY:** | Ha! Ha! |
| **MARVIN:** | Please sir, I'll make it fifty dollars. |
| **BOBBY:** | Fifty dollars? |
| **CHRIS:** | Bobby, it's the chance of a lifetime! |
| **BOBBY:** | You're that afraid of me? |
| **MARVIN:** | Yes. |
| **BOBBY:** | Good. |
| **SAMMY:** | Good. |

*BOBBY moves menancingly towards MARVIN*

| | |
|---|---|
| **CHRIS:** | Come on, Bobby. He's smaller than you. Give the guy a break. |
| **MARVIN:** | Please. |
| **BOBBY:** | Where do you want it? Your arm? |
| **CHRIS:** | Marvin, there's no talking him out of it. It's time to defend ourselves. |
| **BOBBY:** | You in this too? |
| **CHRIS:** | Yup. |
| **BOBBY:** | I'm going to enjoy this. He must be paying you a lot of money. |
| **CHRIS:** | I'm giving it back. It's come down to the principle of the thing. Come on Marvin. |
| **MARVIN:** | Me? |
| **CHRIS:** | We're as ready as we'll ever be. |
| **MARVIN:** | I don't think I can. |
| **CHRIS:** | You'll never get enough money to stop him. He'll just keep taking it and kicking your butt anyway. This way, you and I have a 50/50 chance. |
| **MARVIN:** | Two against two. I guess that's fair. |
| **SAMMY:** | Oh, I'm not fighting. I never fight. I just hold Bobby's jacket while he fights. |

| | |
|---|---|
| **CHRIS:** | How long are you going to let him bully you? |
| **BOBBY:** | Shut up! |
| **SAMMY:** | Yeah, shut up. |
| **BOBBY:** | (*To SAMMY.*) And you shut up too. |
| **SAMMY:** | (*Shocked.*) Hey, Bobby, I was just . . . |
| **BOBBY:** | I said shut up. |
| **MARVIN:** | You gonna take that from him Sammy? You gonna remember that when you're up til midnight doing his homework for him? |
| **SAMMY:** | Bobby, I was just . . . |
| **BOBBY:** | I told you to shut up. |
| **CHRIS:** | This is your chance, Sammy. We could whip him three to one. |
| **MARVIN:** | Come on Sammy! |
| **BOBBY:** | (*Taking off his jacket.*) Here, hold this! |
| **SAMMY:** | Hold it yourself. |
| **BOBBY:** | What? |
| **MARVIN:** | (*With CHRIS.*) All right! |
| **SAMMY:** | I've had enough of this, Bobby. Today it's 3 to 1. |

*ALL freeze.*

**CHRIS:**
I'd rather make him laugh than fight
My hands are sweating, stomach's tight.
My clowning often gets me by
But inside I'm a serious guy.

**MARVIN:**
My money usually paves the way.
But I gotta stand and fight today.
My knees are shaking, hands are clammy
But I didn't have to bribe my buddies Chris and Sammy.

**SAMMY:**
Enough's enough, can't take any more
Why am I being his slave? What for?
At least with two allies I might even survive
Who knows, we might even get through this alive.

**BOBBY:**
I thought they'd back off
Get nervous, cold feet
But now it's 3 to 1
And I'm really dead meat.

I'm biggest, so bully's the role that I play.
Do you think that they'll like me if I change my ways?

**ALL BOYS:** Do you like me?

                      ❧   ❧   ❧

**SARAH:** Listen, I don't have time to talk to you now. I've got a book report and three pages of math. Then I'm doing two extra credit projects. Are you kidding? I've got to watch my grades. I've never been less than an A average student. I don't intend to ever do less. Of course the other kids don't understand that. They call me nerd and teacher's pet. Never mind. My first year in Harvard and they'll still be doing 7th grade math! I don't have time for childhood. I don't have time for silly birthday parties and sleepovers and children's games. In today's competitive world, adults are the only ones who can afford to act like children. My parents have high expectations. What would happen if I told them I needed some time to relax and do baby things — like ride on a swing, or jump in a swimming pool? Would they like me?

                            ða   ða   ða

**GIRLS:** Do you like me?
Do you like me?
Do you see how important that question can be?

**BOYS:** What we feel inside and what we show out
Can be two different things
That's what this play's about.

**ALL:** We wanted to show you
Really wanted you to know.
We hope that you liked us
And also liked our show.

## The End.

# BY MYSELF, ALONE

## Introduction

The theme I wanted to explore in this play was that of aloneness: what is it like, those times when you are by yourself, or you stand out like a sore themb? I gave my students the following assignment: "Next week when you come to class, I want you to be able to describe to us a situation in which you found yourself alone, or standing out in the crowd. Be able to tell us what happened and how you felt about it. Also tell me what name you'd like your character to have."

The next session was enlightening and touching. I was fascinated to hear that being alone in the house still frightened them sometimes, no matter how grown up they think they are. I learned (or rather was reminded) how awful you feel not having a partner for the class trip, or being left out of the in-group because you're wearing the wrong clothes. I took frantic notes while the kids spoke to one another, then came back with a script a week later. I didn't match each student with his/her own story because I didn't want the play that heavily autobiographical. I wanted it to be more of a general statement for the performers.

Because this play was written for students in Black Kids in Theatre, my own theatre group, two of the pieces, Scenes Three and Four, are specifically for black performers. The other scenes and monologues may be played by any and all performers.

I staged this without sets, props, lights, music, or costumes. Other than the performers, the only things on stage were nine chairs. For the opening, we lined them up across the stage. The curtains opened and each student was frozen in a pose that reflected his/her character's personality. The choral pieces were written to bond the group, but also to serve as transitions and cover the scene changes, as we arranged the chairs to become school bus seats and classroom desks, and removed them for the gym and the soccer game. In Scene Seven, the rest of the cast said goodbye to Jenny and the curtain closed. Jenny sat on the apron of the stage. The cast whispered from behind the curtain, and eventually poked their heads out from underneath the curtain behind her. Jenny never looked at them, but it became very funny for the audience.

In the last scene, the cast brought their chairs onstage and hid behind them to become the imaginary creatures and noisemakers that frighten Abby in the house by herself. On her line, "Oh great, there's the car, and yippee it's my folks," the cast faded off backstage, taking their chairs.

For the ending, the students used the last lines as a rap.

## Cast

| | |
|---|---|
| **Anna** | **Abby** |
| **Billy Joe** | **Jane** |
| **Diana** | **Jenny** |
| **JR** | **Corey** |
| **Katherine** | |

| ANNA: | Sitting in the classroom, surrounded by my friends |
| | Kids with me side by side, my buddies end to end |
| BILLY JOE: | Sitting in the classroom with all the other guys |
| | We're just about the same shape and almost the same size. |
| DIANA: | Sitting in the classroom with all my girlfriends who |
| | Like to wear the same clothes and do the same things too. |
| JR: | Sitting in the classroom but I just can't unwind |
| | 'Cause I'm so full of feelings, got plenty on my mind. |
| KATHERINE: | There are moments in a group when I can feel so lonely |
| | Though I'm one of many, I feel just like an only |
| ABBY: | Sometimes it's really great to stand out from the crowd |
| | Sometimes it's so embarrassing I want to shout out loud. |
| JANE: | Sometimes alone means special, it means that you're the best |
| | Sometimes it means that you're a nerd |
| | To stand out from the rest. |
| JENNY: | I don't mind being by myself those moments that I choose |
| | But when I'm forced to be alone, I really feel the blues. |
| COREY: | We'd like to show you how we feel, we'd like it to be known |
| | What happens to us, what we do, when we really feel alone. |

## Scene One

| KATHERINE: | What time will the bus get here? |
| JENNY: | 9:15 and I can't wait. |
| ANNA: | I've been to the bathroom 15 times. I don't want to miss a minute of scenery on the bus. |
| JENNY: | But remember, I get the window seat. |
| COREY: | I've got ten bucks. I hope we stop at the gift shop. |
| BILLY JOE: | And Miss Keller better let us look around. I want to buy a lot. |
| DIANA: | I hope the restaurant has chicken salad sandwiches. |
| ABBY: | If you order that, I'll get a cheeseburger and we can trade halves. |
| JANE: | Hey Katherine, you can sit by the window on the way. |
| KATHERINE: | And you take it on the way back. |
| JR: | How do you two know you're sitting together? |
| JANE: | (With KATHERINE.) We're partners. |
| JR: | Who says? |
| JANE: | (With KATHERINE.) Miss Keller. |
| ABBY: | We chose partners yesterday. Miss Keller said we could pick whoever we wanted. |
| JR: | But I was absent yesterday. |

| | |
|---|---|
| **JENNY:** | So. Partners are already assigned. |
| **JR:** | (*To COREY.*) Who are you with? |
| **COREY:** | Billy Joe. |
| **JR:** | Who's with Jack? |
| **BILLY JOE:** | Jack's with Tommy and Greg got Calvin. |
| **JR:** | What about me? |
| **DIANA:** | Kim doesn't have a partner. You could sit with her. |
| **ALL:** | Oooooooooh! |
| **JR:** | Cut it out you guys. I'm not sitting with a *girl!* |
| **ANN:** | Well the girls don't want to sit with you either! |
| **JR:** | (*To COREY and BILLY JOE.*) Can I just hang out with you two? |
| **BILLY JOE:** | The seats only hold two people. |
| **JENNY:** | And Miss Keller said pick *one* partner, not two. Come on, Anna. Let's get in the front of the line. |

*They pair up.*

| | |
|---|---|
| **COREY:** | Hey, Billy Joe, let's sit all the way in the back. |

*They pair up.*

| | |
|---|---|
| **JANE:** | (*With KATHERINE.*) We're sitting in the front! (*They pair off.*) |
| **JR:** | So everybody had a partner except me. Who'd I get to sit next to? Miss Keller. |
| **ALL:** | Oooooh. |
| **JR:** | Instead of playing checkers and trading Micro machines with a buddy, I had to listen to two hours of facts about the early settlers. For lunch Miss Keller orders a tossed salad. Who wants to trade halves for that? It wasn't all bad, I guess. She did buy me a bag of Doritos and I could eat every last one without sharing. But the ride back was so boring, I just fell asleep. Calvin and Greg got separated for fighting over a Hershey bar. Katherine and Jane got yelled at for screaming over pictures of Malcolm Jamal Warner in a teen magazine. And Billy Joe and Corey got in trouble for stuffing Kim's sweater in the toilet. I stayed out of trouble for once and got a sticker from Miss Keller. But I'll never be absent before a field trip again. I don't ever want to go on a trip without a partner. Who cares about the early settlers or a bag of Doritos for yourself? If you don't have a partner, it's just no fun! |
| **ALL:** | No need to sulk, no need to pout<br>Everybody has a time when they feel left out.<br>You may have to go on the trip alone<br>But you still had your friends when you got back home. |

🐌 🐌 🐌

## Scene Two

**BILLY JOE:** (*To COREY.*) Hey man, what are you wearing?

**COREY:** What do you mean?

**JR:** Clothes! What do you think!

**BILLY JOE:** What kind of pants are those?

**JR:** What day is today?

**COREY:** Are you guys weird or something?

**BILLY JOE:** It's Friday, Corey!

**JR:** You know our club passed a rule.

**BILLY JOE:** Every Friday, all the guys in the club have to wear Bugle Boys.

**COREY:** Well, I forgot, OK?

**JR:** You forgot last Friday too.

**COREY:** Big deal. It's a skateboard club anyway. Who cares what you wear?

**BILLY JOE:** But it's the club rule. And if you can't follow the rules . . .

**JR:** You're out of the club!

> *JR and BILLY JOE exit.*

**COREY:** (*To Audience.*) I'm the only one in the club who doesn't have a pair of Bugle Boys. I'm probably the only one in the world who doesn't have a pair of Bugle Boys. They're these really cool pants. Some have ribs down them. Some have cuffs with flannel designs on them. They're awesome. And it's Friday. Of all the days to have to get up in front of class and do a math problem and read my English composition. Every time I stand up, I'm gonna feel the club guys looking at me. I keep telling them I forget, but I don't have any. Dad says $30.00 is too much for pants I'm going to put a hole in anyway. Mom says the only thing awesome about Bugle Boys is the price. Say, maybe if I cut up my flannel pajamas with the designs and sew them on the cuffs of my regular pants, they'd look like Bugle Boys! No, I guess not. I'm the only boy in my class without Bugle Boys. I'm desperate!

**ALL:**
Clubs are great when you're the boss
But when you're out, you're at a loss
The whole thing's dumb, everybody knows
They shouldn't kick you out just because of your clothes.

🐸 🐸 🐸

## Scene Three

| | |
|---|---|
| **JANE:** | I just couldn't believe it. I thought I had imagined it. Then the teacher said it again. |
| **KATHERINE:** | (*As the teacher.*) Boys and girls we are very lucky that Jane's mother is coming in this afternoon to tell us all about Africa. |
| **JANE:** | Oh no! I told my mother specifically, I begged her. Please don't come to school anymore. Please don't get up in front of all my friends and go on and on like you always do. |
| **KATHERINE:** | Jane's mother is going to bring slides and cloth and samples of African food. |
| **JANE:** | Oh Mom, don't bring out those same old slides. Don't bring the yam balls! The kids will think they're yucky! |
| **ABBY:** | I love to taste new things. |
| **JANE:** | It's boring. I eat it all the time. |
| **DIANA:** | I don't. Besides, I'd much rather have an hour of your mother than an hour of school work. |
| **JANE:** | But it's so embarrassing. |
| **JENNY:** | What's so embarrassing? |
| **JANE:** | She's just . . . I don't know . . . she's just . . . here. |
| **ABBY:** | So what? |
| **JANE:** | Cake sales,book fairs. PTA. She's *always* in school. |
| **ANNA:** | So's my Mom, but that's because I'm always in trouble. |
| **DIANA:** | So what if she comes to school. The teachers like her. |
| **JENNY:** | Yeah, so they like you more. |
| **JANE:** | I don't want the teachers to like me. I want to be just like everybody else. |
| **KATHERINE:** | And Jane's mother has promised to demonstrate the African dance she studies. We'll all get to play the drums and the bells! |
| **CLASS:** | All right! Cool! Awesome! |
| **JANE:** | I could just die! |
| **ABBY:** | You're so lucky your Mom comes in. Mine works all the time. |
| **JANE:** | Lucky! Yeah, sure! Drums, bells, African dance? Oh no! Now, don't get me wrong. I love my mother. She can be cool about once every three years. Why does she have to be so . . . unusual? She comes in here and draws attention to me. All the kids look at me. She expects me to get up in front of the class. And then, when she's gone, I get all the dumb comments. Mom just says (*Imitating her mother.*) "That's just ignorance, Jane. That's exactly why I come to school to teach the children about Africa so they won't say those stupid things." But in the lunchroom, at recess I have to deal with the jerks all alone. I don't want to be different. I don't want to be special. I don't want my Mom in the classroom turning the spotlight on me. |

45

| ALL: | Explain to your Mom what happens in school |
|---|---|
| | You don't want to be special, you want to be cool! |
| | Let her know you appreciate the things that she does |
| | But ask her not to come as often as she was. |

&#10086; &#10086; &#10086;

## Scene Four

**BILLY JOE:** You think you stand out! Look at me. For as long as I can remember, I've been the tallest boy in my class.

**JR:** Better to be the tallest than the shortest!

**BILLY JOE:** No way! In gym class . . .

*Everyone does jumping jacks.*

**COREY:** (*Acting like a teacher.*) You there! You, the tall boy . . . stop that talking!

**BILLY JOE:** When trouble's brewing, they can always spot me in a crowd. The only place I could blend in is at the National Basketball Academy.

**ABBY:** (*Imitating a grown-up.*) You're too old to act so silly!

**BILLY JOE:** Everyone always thinks I'm older than I am. 14, 15, even a short 16.

**JR:** People think I'm 8. You think that's fun?

**BILLY JOE:** Yeah, because if you act your age they think you're wonderfully mature and sophisticated. But I'm tall. I'm always trying to measure up to their expectations. And the kids tease me, too.

**DIANA:** Hey bean pole!

**JENNY:** Hey, Manute Boll!

**ABBY:** How's the weather up there?

**ANNA:** You've got clouds in your hair.

**BILLY JOE:** Maybe I'll stop growing. Do you think? That way everyone will catch up with me. Maybe I'll even end up the shortest. What would that be like?

*He acts out the other people.*

"Hey, I'll get that for you dear, you can't reach it." "You're so mature for your size young man!" "Hey you big girls, stop picking on Billy Joe, or I'll report you to the principal!" Ah, wouldn't that be great? Of course being tall has some advantages. I can always see in the movies. I drive the kids behind me nuts. I'm in the back row in the choir. We trade marbles and have a blast with 25 kids in front to cover us. And on the night of the performance, when I sing like an angel, I'm easy to spot. "Who's that tall, handsome young man in the back row? He really stands out!" Yeah, I guess I'll stay like I am. A head above the rest. It's not a bad place to be.

46

**ALL:** You may be the exception, not the rule
But take it from us, brother, tall is cool!
Don't let them upset you, better get wise
Be who you are, 'cause you're just the right size!

ᘓ ᘓ ᘓ

## Scene Five

**ANNA:** There were five of us. All good friends, all enjoying a fine summmer Saturday. Sarah had an awesome house with an awesome pool, so we decided to swim. I jumped in with my buddies and splashed around for about an hour. Then we sat poolside and played with our Barbie dolls. It was great until Beth suddenly screamed and pointed at me. "Oh look!" "What, get it off! Get it offf!" I thought a bug was on me. Then Sarah screams, "Look at your hair!" I brushed at my hair in panic. I thought it was a bee or a wasp. Then "Your hair is so gigantic!" Mavis says. Well, I feel my head and sure enough, my barrettes had come off in the pool. Now when my hair gets wet and then dry, it frizzes up and gets real big. That's just the way it is. But the way my friends were acting, you'd think King Kong had popped out of my skull. "How are you going to get it back to the way it was?" asked Sarah. That was a good question, because my Mom's in charge of the hair department. I ended up real mad because my friends kept asking dumb questions and pointing at me. When they tried to see if Barbie could stand up in my hair, I phoned Mom to come and take me home.

**DIANA:** Was that the end of your friendships?

**ANNA:** Oh no. We're all still buddies. As a matter of fact, they think my hair is awesome. They wish they had hair like Whitney Houston like I do.

**ALL:** Your hair, your nose, your skin color too
May be different from the kids who hang around with you
Respect what's different about eacah other
'Cause we're also the same, like sister and brother.

ᘓ ᘓ ᘓ

## Scene Six

*Boys are having an imaginary soccer game. KATHERINE plays. The other girls watch.*

**JR:** Over here, I'm open!

**COREY:** Pass it quick!

**KATHERINE:** I got it. I got it!

**PLAYERS:** (*Together.*) GOAL! GOAL! Awesome, we got it!

**JENNY:** Hey, Katherine, why don't you play with us?

| | |
|---|---|
| **ABBY:** | Hey, Katherine, why don't you play with the girls for a change? |
| **ANNA:** | Hey Katherine, you look just like a boy! |
| **DIANA:** | Hey Katherine, you sure you're not a boy? |

*They laugh in a mean way.*

| | |
|---|---|
| **BILLY JOE:** | Don't pay them any attention. |
| **COREY:** | Yeah, they're just jealous. |
| **JR:** | Way to go, Katherine. You won the game! |
| **JANE:** | But girls aren't supposed to play with the boys. |
| **ABBY:** | Girls aren't supposed to get all sweaty and dirty. |
| **JENNY:** | Girls aren't supposed to run around and act like maniacs. |
| **KATHERINE:** | I'll punch your lights out! |
| **ANNA:** | And girls are not supposed to fight like little hoodlums! No wonder none of the girls will be your friends. |
| **KATHERINE:** | I don't need any girl friends. I think you're a bunch of sissies. I have plenty of guys for my buddies. |
| **JR:** | Yo guys, let's go to my house. |
| **COREY:** | O.K., let's go. |
| **KATHERINE:** | Yeah, I'll race you. |
| **JR:** | Not now, Katherine. This is just for the guys. |
| **COREY:** | Hey, we like you Katherine, but . . . |
| **JR:** | This is for boys only. |
| **KATHERINE:** | So here I am. Caught between two sides. Unwanted by either. The girls have their little close groups with secrets and partie and sleepovers. They don't invite me. The boys think I'm great on the soccer field, but when it comes to ther clubs, they won't let me in. I try to act like it doesn't matter. What else can I do? (*Indicating boys.*) If they think I'm going to beg them, they can forget it! (*Indicating girls.*) If they think I'm going to let them see me cry, they can go jump in a lake! But what am I going to do? |
| **ABBY:** | Pssst, Katherine? |
| **KATHERINE:** | What do you want? |
| **ABBY:** | You know, if you wouldn't act so tough and BAAAD all the time, we'd love to have you play with us. Most of the girls think you're kind of cool. But you always have an attitude. |
| **JR:** | Psst, Katherine? |
| **KATHERINE:** | Huh? |
| **JR:** | The guys don't want to hurt your feelings. It's just that sometimes we need to be by ourselves. |
| **KATHERINE:** | So, it looks like both sides want me, but in different ways. Maybe I can do both. |
| **ALL:** | You don't have to be lonely without a friend in the world You ought to split your time between the boys and the girls. |

| | |
|---|---|
| **GIRLS:** | Play soccer with the guys but when the game ends |
| **BOYS:** | Make sure you take a time out with your girlfriends. |

&a   &a   &a

## Scene Seven

| | |
|---|---|
| **JENNY:** | Girls vs. girls. Boys vs. boys. Girls vs. boys and on and on. Every day it's back and forth. Who's cool vs. who's a nerd? Who's in between? Who cares! I tell you something, when 3:00 rolls around, I'm so happy to get off that school bus. |
| **ALL:** | Bye Jenny. See you tomorrow. Call you later. |
| | *They exit.* |
| **JENNY:** | And I can't wait to hit my front door. |
| | *She knocks on an imaginary front door.* |
| | I'm going to have a grilled cheese sandwich and a big glass of chocolate milk. (*She knocks again.*) I'm going to kick off my shoes, flop down on the couch and watch "Silver Spoons." (*She knocks harder and shouts.*) Hey! I'm home! Mom? Mom? I'm home! |
| **ALL:** | (*Whispering from backstage.*) No answer. |
| **JENNY:** | Oh darn it. |
| **ALL:** | Nobody's home. |
| **JENNY:** | It's 3:30. Mom's supposed to be here. |
| **ALL:** | What are you going to do? |
| **JENNY:** | Mom always says if she's not home to just sit on the steps and wait. |
| **ALL:** | Go to a neighbor's. |
| **JENNY:** | Then she won't know where I am. |
| **ALL:** | You're going to sit here all alone? |
| **JENNY:** | I'll be all right. |
| | *Pause.* |
| **ALL:** | What time is it now? |
| **JENNY:** | 3:45. |
| **ALL:** | Seems more like 5:00, doesn't it? |
| **JENNY:** | She'll be here soon. |
| **ALL:** | You hope! |
| | *Pause.* |
| **ALL:** | What time is it now? |
| **JENNY:** | It's 4:00! |
| **ALL:** | How are you feeling? |

| | |
|---|---|
| **JENNY:** | Angry. Why didn't she leave a note? I hate this. She always tells me to be responsible. What about her? |
| | *Pause.* |
| **ALL:** | What time is it now? |
| **JENNY:** | (*Almost in tears.*) 4:15! |
| **ALL:** | How are you feeling now? |
| **JENNY:** | All alone. |
| **ALL:** | And scared! |
| **JENNY:** | What if she never comes back? What if a stranger comes along and grabs me? What if it gets dark and cold and I have no food? What if I pass out from starvation right here on my own front steps. (*She starts to cry.*) |
| **ALL:** | Jenny, look! |
| **JENNY:** | (*Sobbing.*) Leave me alone! |
| **ALL:** | But look, it's your Mom! |
| **JENNY:** | (*Jumps up, yelling at an imaginary Mom.*) Mom! Mom! Where the heck have you been? No, I wasn't crying. Just resting my eyes. |
| **ALL:** | We know it's rough, we know it's not breezy<br>But when you're waiting alone, just try to take it easy.<br>When your mother is running a little bit late<br>Just try not to panic and keep thinking straight. |

&#10086; &#10086; &#10086;

## Scene Eight

| | |
|---|---|
| **DIANA:** | (*To audience.*) They all act as if being alone is the worst thing in the world. It doesn't have to be. When I'm by myself, alone, I have a wonderful time. I'm quite happy to have *my* clothes, *my* books, *my* toys, *my* room. All to myself. I have my friends over all the time. Sure, I've got a zillion cousins who spend Christmas and summer vacations. They try on my clothes and play with my favorite stuff. I manage to smile and I do enjoy their company. And when I say goodbye, I even feel a little lonely. My room is quiet again. Nobody to laugh at my Bill Cosby imitation. Nobody to play Uno with me. But then I remember that my Dad's lap will be all mine when I need a hug. And I'll get to lick the Brownie batter bowl all by myself. And when I snuggle down in my *own* bed, in my *own* room, with my *own* favorite doll beside me, it's actually quite delicious to be by myself alone. |
| **ALL:** | Being alone is not a crime<br>You can often have quite a wonderful time.<br>Snacking, relaxing, daydreaming of glory<br>But when it's at night, it's a different story! |

&#10086; &#10086; &#10086;

# Scene Nine

| | |
|---|---|
| **ABBY:** | My Mom, Dad and brother just walked out the door<br>They've left me alone while they ran to the store.<br>I told they I'd stay home, I will for a lark<br>But after they drive off, I realize . . . |
| **ALL:** | It's dark! |
| **ABBY:** | Quick, put on the TV for noise and for light<br>I scoop up my Garfield and hug him real tight.<br>Close all the curtains 'cause outside looks black<br>Head to the kitchen to get a big snack.<br>All of the goodies Mom won't let me eat<br>I get them all out and I feast, what a treat!<br>But what's that, a noise and it came from upstairs<br>It could be a killer, or monster, or bears!<br>I'm not going up there, no way babe, not me<br>And if it comes downstairs, I'll bash it and flee! |
| **ALL:** | Don't think about it. |
| **ABBY:** | You're right, I'll calm down<br>I'll whistle a tune and I'll dance all around.<br>I'll play the piano, while I'm reading a book<br>Whatever is in here, I'm not going to look.<br>I'm going to sing opera, and hide under the couch.<br>It's safe, but my hair's caught. Help! Get me out! OUCH!<br>I'll talk to myself, yes, I'll tell myself jokes.<br>Oh great there's the car, and yippie, it's my folks!<br>I'm awfully, so very glad that they're home<br>Next time I'll go with them and not stay alone! |
| **JENNY:** | So this is our story |
| **JR:** | In rap and in rhyme. |
| **DIANA:** | We hope that you like it |
| **ANNA:** | And had a good time. |
| **JANE:** | So next time you're lonely |
| **KATHERINE:** | Or face the unknown |
| **ABBY:** | Don't worry, don't panic . . . |
| **BILLY JOE:** | Feeling left on your own. |
| **COREY:** | Be brave, have the courage, stand solo alone |
| **ALL:** | Be brave, by yourself, stand up solo, alone! |

# The End.

# SCENES FOR PAIRS AND TRIOS

## Introduction

My goals in creating these scenes were the same as those in creating the plays: giving students substantive, reality-based roles that would give them an opportunity to explore social issues as well as character choices.

I am intrigued, both as a director and teacher, by role reversals (When does the weak character become the strong one? When does the "bad guy" become the "good guy"?) and problem resolution (How can two people work out their problems; how can they communicate what may be painful to articulate?) Some of the scenes deal with conflict of characters, others with classroom dynamics and social hierarchy and status. Scenes centered around larger social issues, which may serve as a springboard to discussion, are

- Keep in a Safe, Dry Place
- Tell Herman
- Rainbow Girls
- In Common.

Should you wish to put these scenes together for a program, consider asking your students to find common themes, personal experiences and/or descriptions which could then be worked into a linking narrative. Or you may ask them to find music highlighting some of the themes of the pieces.

## DON'T WANNA

### A Scene for Two Girls

*Sally's room. SALLY reads.*

| | |
|---|---|
| **PRU:** | This is boring. |
| **SALLY:** | Watch TV. |
| **PRU:** | Nah, don't wanna. |
| **SALLY:** | Play my Bon Jovi tape. |
| **PRU:** | Nah, that's corny. |
| **SALLY:** | There are some games in my closet. |
| **PRU:** | Nah, that's dumb. |
| **SALLY:** | We can go outside and ride bikes. |
| **PRU:** | Nah. |
| **SALLY:** | Well, there's some paper and markers if you want to draw. |
| **PRU:** | Draw what? |
| **SALLY:** | How should I know — people, houses, popsicles! |

| | |
|---|---|
| PRU: | You're such a baby. (*Pause.*) You still read those Nancy Drew mysteries? |
| SALLY: | Yeah. |
| PRU: | You actually like them? |
| SALLY: | Get off my case will you? |
| PRU: | I'm just asking a question. |
| SALLY: | Listen, what's your problem, Toots? |
| PRU: | Toots? That's dumb. |
| SALLY: | Yeah, exactly. I'd like to call you something worse but I'm afraid my Mom would hear. |
| PRU: | I'm going to tell her you're threatening me. |
| SALLY: | Fine, we'll both go. You tell her that and I'll tell her you've been a pain in my . . . neck for the past two hours. You don't want to watch TV or go outside or draw or read or listen to music. You don't want to do anything. No wonder all the kids call you . . . |

*She suddenly covers her hand over her mouth.*

| | |
|---|---|
| PRU: | All the kids call me what? |
| SALLY: | Nothing. Never mind. |
| PRU: | All the kids call me what? |
| SALLY: | They call you a name. |
| PRU: | They do not. You're lying. (*Pause.*) What name? |
| SALLY: | "Pru-Pru the Pooh-Pooh." |
| PRU: | What! I'm telling your mother. |
| SALLY: | That's why! Because you're always telling on people. You're always pooh-pooh-ing on something. |

*Imitates PRU.*

"Nah, I don't wanna." "This is dumb." "This is boring." You never laugh. You never want to get excited and have fun. All you want to do is act like a major drag.

| | |
|---|---|
| PRU: | You want me to spas out like you. |

*Imitates SALLY.*

"Oh goody, goody gum drops, wowsers, yippee!"

| | |
|---|---|
| SALLY: | I don't act like that. |
| PRU: | Well pretty close. If your life was like mine you'd do nothing but cry. |
| SALLY: | You think you're the only one who has it tough? |
| PRU: | My parents are never home. My brother beats me up. I have no friends and I'm flunking out of school. |
| SALLY: | Oh yeah, real tough! My heart bleeds for you. Listen, Toots, my parents have split up, my sister ran away, we're going to have to move because my Mom |

can't afford this house, and my dog died last week! So don't tell me about your rough life!

PRU: Are you kidding?

SALLY: Do I look like I'm kidding?

PRU: Gee, I didn't know.

SALLY: No, 'cause I don't go around dragging everybody down with my problems. I deal with them. I ride my bike, jump around to Ben Jovi and escape into mystery stories and drawing.

PRU: You're really going to have to move?

SALLY: I don't wanna talk about it.

PRU: Okay, okay. I just wanted to say that . . . I'm going to miss you. You've been nicer to me than anybody else. (*Pause.*) You wanna ride bikes?

SALLY: Hey, now that's something, Toots! Pru- Pru the Pooh-Pooh on a bike. This I gotta see!

❧ ❧ ❧

# TRAITOR
## A Scene for Two Boys and One Girl

STEVE: Want to play another game of Nintendo?

CHUCK: Nah, my eyeballs are falling out.

STEVE: I wish it wasn't raining.

CHUCK: Me too.

> *JAN enters.*

STEVE: What do you want, dog breath?

JAN: None of your business, weasel brain.

STEVE: Beat it, horse lips.

JAN: Make me, frog eyes.

> *She sits down and turns on the TV.*

CHUCK: (*Pulling on STEVE's sleeve.*) Is that your sister?

STEVE: Yeah. I hate her guts.

JAN: The feeling's mutual, slime ball.

CHUCK: (*Pulling on STEVE's sleeve.*) She's in Mrs. Nader's class right?

STEVE: Yeah. (*To JAN.*) You have to get out because I have company.

JAN: Eat dirt.

CHUCK: (*Pulls on STEVE's sleeve.*) She's Myra Kinney's best friend, right?

STEVE: I don't know. (*To JAN.*) How'd ya like toothpaste inside your new Reeboks?

| | |
|---|---|
| JAN: | How'd ya like to ride a skateboard with no wheels? |
| CHUCK: | (*Pulls on STEVE's sleeve.*) Ask her if she's Myra Kinney's friend. |
| STEVE: | Look, what is your problem? |
| CHUCK: | Ask her. |
| STEVE: | Cut it out. Ask her yourself. |
| JAN: | Will you two mutants keep it down? I'm trying to look at this. |
| CHUCK: | (*Shy at first.*) Uh . . . excuse me . . . Uh . . . do you know Myra Kinney? |
| JAN: | What? |
| CHUCK: | You know Myra Kinney, right? |
| JAN: | Duh, Sherlock. She's only my best friend. |
| CHUCK: | Oh. |
| JAN: | Why do you want to know? |
| STEVE: | Yeah, what do you care? |
| CHUCK: | Oh nothing. No reason. |
| JAN: | You're Chuck, right? I'll tell Myra you were asking for her. |
| CHUCK: | (*Suddenly scared.*) Oh don't. Please don't! |
| STEVE: | Chill out, man. What's your problem. |
| JAN: | Can't you see, pig face? Your friend likes Myra. |
| CHUCK: | I don't! I don't! |
| JAN: | Then why are you sweating and turning colors? |
| CHUCK: | I don't like her. Honest. |
| STEVE: | Hey, buzzard beak, he doesn't like her! You don't, do you? |
| CHUCK: | Not really. |
| JAN: | So how come you're always watching her at recess? |
| STEVE: | You don't, do you Chuck? |
| JAN: | So how come you make goo-goo eyes at her on the bus and hang around her seat? |
| STEVE: | He does not. Tell me you don't, Chuck! |
| CHUCK: | She dropped her pencil on the bus. I picked it up, that's all. |
| STEVE: | Oh no! Oh no! |
| JAN: | (*At the same time.*) See, see I told you! |
| CHUCK: | Don't tell her I like her. PLEEEEZ! |
| STEVE: | Not you too. You and Eric and Mike make me sick with this love business. |
| JAN: | You're just jealous because nobody likes you, buffalo breath. |
| STEVE: | I don't like anybody. And I don't want anybody to like me. Just because you want to marry Raymond Harris |
| JAN: | (*Shouting.*) Shut up! I don't. I don't even know him. |
| CHUCK: | I do. He lives next door to me. |

| | |
|---|---|
| **JAN:** | (*Swoops down on CHUCK.*) He does! What's he like? Does he go to the park? Does he have a girlfriend? |
| **CHUCK:** | Well, I'll tell you about Ray if you tell me about Myra. |
| **STEVE:** | I'm gonna throw up! What's the matter with you people? We're too young for this love garbage. |
| **JAN:** | Well some of us are obviously more mature than others. Come Charles, shall we retire to the kitchen where we can talk about two very important people? |
| **CHUCK:** | I'll see you in a while, Steve. |
| | *They exit.* |
| **STEVE:** | That's right. Go on and leave me over some dumb girl. The whole class is going nuts. I'm the last guy in my class who hates girls. Even old Chuck's a traitor now. What's going to happen to me? |

             ٮ    ٮ    ٮ

## COOL BUT TROUBLE
### A Scene for Two Girls

| | |
|---|---|
| **CLAIRE:** | Hey, how ya doin'? |
| **WENDY:** | I'm cool. |
| **CLAIRE:** | You certainly are. You were really incredible. |
| **WENDY:** | Yeah. |
| **CLAIRE:** | I mean it. You were unbelievable. |
| **WENDY:** | Yeah. |
| **CLAIRE:** | Your reputation is spreading like wildfire. All the kids are talking about you. |
| **WENDY:** | What are they saying? |
| **CLAIRE:** | How you told Miss O'Connell you didn't have your homework because you just didn't do it. |
| **WENDY:** | Check it out. |
| **CLAIRE:** | Because homework is dumb anyhow and how you could learn more by watching TV. |
| **WENDY:** | Exactly. |
| **CLAIRE:** | And that no one in the world could make you do your homework if you didn't want to. |
| **WENDY:** | Bet to that. |
| **CLAIRE:** | And how this is a free country and you are free under the Constitution. |
| **WENDY:** | All right. I guess I told her. |

| | |
|---|---|
| **CLAIRE:** | Wow! |
| **WENDY:** | Thanks. |
| **CLAIRE:** | So what happens now? |
| **WENDY:** | O'Connell called my mom. |
| **CLAIRE:** | Uh-oh. |
| **WENDY:** | No problem. I can handle it. As long as I know the class is behind me. |
| **CLAIRE:** | Oh, they are. |
| **WENDY:** | Face it, when you're a leader, you have to take risks. |
| **CLAIRE:** | Wow. |
| **WENDY:** | I wish she hadn't sent me out. I wish I could have been there to see the whole class protesting. |
| **CLAIRE:** | Huh? |
| **WENDY:** | Like we agreed. Everybody just refused to do homework, right? |
| **CLAIRE:** | Uh . . . um . . . |
| **WENDY:** | So O'Connell sent you to the office too right? Is she going to call your mom too? |
| **CLAIRE:** | Well, actually, no. |
| **WENDY:** | Well, what did O'Connell do when the whole class went on homework strike? |
| **CLAIRE:** | They didn't. |
| **WENDY:** | What happened to the protest? What happened after O'Connell hollered at me and sent me to the office? |
| **CLAIRE:** | Everybody just shut up and finished copying down tonight's homework. |
| **WENDY:** | But I was the leader. |
| **CLAIRE:** | You sure were. |
| **WENDY:** | But nobody followed. |
| **CLAIRE:** | Gee, sorry about that. But I want you to know that we all think you're really cool. See you! |
| | *Exits.* |
| **WENDY:** | My Mom's gonna skin me alive! |

&#10087;  &#10087;  &#10087;

# KEEP IN A SAFE, DRY PLACE
## A Scene for Two Boys

**BILLY:** Don't worry, I'll protect you.

**SID:** You?

**BILLY:** Yeah.

**SID:** I'm in for it now.

**BILLY:** You don't believe I can, but I will. We'll be perfectly safe, Sid. I know a place where we can hide for days.

**SID:** Sure, without food, money or blankets.

**BILLY:** We'll find a way.

**SID:** Your trouble is, you read too many of those ridiculous Sir Lancelot stories. You don't even know the difference between make believe and real life any more.

**BILLY:** I know we don't have to take that garbage Zack gives us all the time. He's not even our legal guardian.

**SID:** Tell that to the cops!

**BILLY:** I will and a whole lot more. I'll go to the courts if I have to.

**SID:** Listen you jerk, before you get all hyped up and run off to the People's Court, let me give you the facts: we're non-adoptables. Nobody wants us. We're foster kids. Somebody's makin' money off of us. And you just hit our temporary caretaker over the head with a frying pan. Everybody's looking for us.

**BILLY:** I just couldn't take him hitting me anymore.

**SID:** We're walking trouble, you and me. (*Pause.*) Hey, I know Zack stinks. But the street stinks worse. You think we're going to run off into the magic forest and set up in some abandoned castle? We're looking at cement pillows here, Billy Boy. And a storm's blowing up too. At least at Zack's we get three meals and a warm place to sleep. At least there we're out of the rain.

**BILLY:** Is that all you want, Sid? A place to keep dry? Heck, even dogs get more than that.

**SID:** Lucky dogs.

**BILLY:** Don't do this Sid. Don't give up on me.

**SID:** I'm trying to make you see the truth.

**BILLY:** And don't give me that look. I hate that look.

**SID:** What look?

**BILLY:** That "I'm- lower-than-a-dog-so-go-ahead-and-kick-me" look.

**SID:** Being a kid is like being nothing. No money. No power. No place to belong. No say.

**BILLY:** Make a fist.

| | |
|---|---|
| **SID:** | What? |
| **BILLY:** | I said make a fist. |
| **SID:** | (*Makes a fist.*) Yeah? |
| **BILLY:** | Make it strong. |
| **SID:** | Yeah |
| **BILLY:** | (*Puts up his palm.*) Now punch. Right here. |
| **SID:** | You flipped? |
| **BILLY:** | Come on. As hard as you can. |

*SID aims several strong punches into BILLY's hand.*

| | |
|---|---|
| | How did that feel? |
| **SID:** | Great, can I do your face now? |
| **BILLY:** | No. Now you hold up your palm. |
| **SID:** | Wait a minute. |
| **BILLY:** | Go ahead. |

*SID holds up his palm reluctantly. BILLY aims several strong punches into his palm. SID takes the blows but is relieved when they stop.*

| | |
|---|---|
| **SID:** | Ow! Ow! What's the matter with you anyway? You losing your mind or something? |
| **BILLY:** | No. And that's what keeps me from losing my mind. Did you feel my punches? |
| **SID:** | (*Still rubbing his hand.*) What do you think? |
| **BILLY:** | Good. That means you can still feel, Sid. That means your body don't like being punched and kicked and it lets you know. I've seen kids who couldn't feel anymore. That's what scares me. |
| **SID:** | But listen Billy . . . |
| **BILLY:** | Kids too scared to fight back. Too scared to keep on living and looking for something better. |
| **SID:** | But there's no way . . . |
| **BILLY:** | You punch hard, Sid. That's good. That means you still have power. |
| **SID:** | Some power . . . we're only 13. |
| **BILLY:** | Doesn't matter. I've seen people twice our age who couldn't tie their own shoes. We're strong, Sid. We're tough. And we know there's gotta be more to living than staying out of the rain. |

*BILLY walks a few steps. Looks back at SID.*

You coming?

*Pause. SID joins him slowly.*

| | |
|---|---|
| **SID:** | You didn't punch me as hard as I punched you. |
| **BILLY:** | That's O.K. You needed it more than I did. |

## TELL HERMAN
### A Scene for Two Girls

*JEAN packs. SARAH watches.*

| | |
|---|---|
| **SARAH:** | You got everything? |
| **JEAN:** | Yeah. |
| **SARAH:** | You got Herman? |
| **JEAN:** | Nah, I can't take him. |
| **SARAH:** | But I gave him to you. You've got to take him so you can remember me. |
| **JEAN:** | I'll remember you. |
| **SARAH:** | But you've got to take Herman. |
| **JEAN:** | She'd only take him away from me. You keep him and take care of him for me. |
| **SARAH:** | Until you come back. Until you come back, right? |
| **JEAN:** | (*Sarcastically.*) Yeah, right. |
| **SARAH:** | And we'll have a big party, right? We'll dance and have 17 different flavors of Baskin-Robbins. |
| **JEAN:** | Stop. |
| **SARAH:** | Then we'll go out and shoot some firecrackers. |
| **JEAN:** | Shut up! What are you doing this for? Isn't my leaving hard enough? Stop yakking like a dumb, stupid kid. Haven't I taught you anything? Haven't you grown up yet? |
| **SARAH:** | I just wanted to cheer you up. |
| **JEAN:** | What the heck is there to be cheerful about. I'm leaving. |
| **SARAH:** | But you'll be back. |
| **JEAN:** | Your head's like a doggone brick. |
| **SARAH:** | (*On the verge of tears.*) You will be back! You will! |
| **JEAN:** | Shhhh. Shhhh. |
| **SARAH:** | I don't want you to go. |
| **JEAN:** | There's nothing you can do. We've tried all the lawyers and courts and doctors. It's over, Sarah. Now be still. |
| **SARAH:** | They can't make you go back. She's mean and awful to you. |
| **JEAN:** | She's my mother. I have to go. |
| **SARAH:** | Don't you like our family? Don't you want to stay? |
| **JEAN:** | Of course I do. |
| **SARAH:** | Then I won't let you go. I won't. (*She stomps.*) I won't I wont. |

60

| | |
|---|---|
| **JEAN:** | (*Grabbing her.*) Stop acting like a spoiled brat. I mean it. Now sit down and shut up or I'll pop you one! |
| | *SARAH starts crying.* |
| | Come on, come on, quit the bawling. |
| **SARAH:** | It's not fair. |
| **JEAN:** | You just finding that out? The little rich girl makes a discovery. Don't worry, honey, you'll get over it. Your life will go on. You'll grow up here in Ellenwood in your pretty clothes in your pretty room, snuggling up to big soft teddy bears and pigging out on 17 flavors of Baskin Robbins. By this time next year, you won't even remember my face. |
| **SARAH:** | I'll always remember you. I will, I swear! |
| **JEAN:** | (*Sighs.*) Gimme a break! |
| **SARAH:** | I want you to be my big sister and live with us. I'm already missing you so badly I can't stand it. I'll write you every day. I'll call you every night. |
| **JEAN:** | Grow up. She'll be draggin' me from town to town just like before. I won't even have an address, much less a phone. Let me go, Sarah. Forget me. |
| **SARAH:** | (*Almost hysterical.*) No! No! I won't! No! |
| **JEAN:** | Sarah, Sarah, stop it. You're frightening me. Now calm down or I'm going to tell your Mom to take you out of here. |
| | *SARAH begins to calm down. JEAN gets Herman the bear and sits down next to SARAH.* |
| | Now you listen to me. This is very important. Every night before you go to bed, I want you to take Herman here, give him a big hug and whisper a message to me in his ear. I'll hear you. |
| **SARAH:** | That's a big dumb lie. I'm not a baby. |
| **JEAN:** | No, it's true. Herman is my special friend. More special than anyone in the world because you gave him to me. If you love him and hug him and whisper a message to me in his ear, I will hear you. I promise. |
| | *She pauses and listens.* |
| | That's the lawyer's car. I gotta go now. |
| **SARAH:** | But Jean . . . |
| **JEAN:** | Shhhh. Remember what I said. I'll be listening every night. I promise. I'll hear you. |
| | *Exits.* |
| **SARAH:** | I'll never forget you. |

ᗖ ᗖ ᗖ

# SKATE SECRETS
## A Scene for Two Boys

| | |
|---|---|
| **RICKY:** | So you can be on the team? |
| **JT:** | No problem. |
| **RICKY:** | You know how to skate? |
| **JT:** | Are you kidding? |
| **RICKY:** | You can handle a big skateboard? |
| **JT:** | Sure. |
| **RICKY:** | What kind of board do you have? |
| **JT:** | Uh . . . umm . . . what's the best? |
| **RICKY:** | Natas. |
| **JT:** | That's what I've got. |
| **RICKY:** | What's your best move? |
| **JT:** | Name some. |
| **RICKY:** | Ollie, handplant, rail slide. |
| **JT:** | That's it. A rail slide. |
| **RICKY:** | You can rail slide? |
| **JT:** | Yup. |
| **RICKY:** | It took me months to learn that. |
| **JT:** | It did? |
| **RICKY:** | I'm still not real good at it. But with an expert like you on our team, we're going to bury those other guys in the dust! Right? |
| **JT:** | Right. |
| **RICKY:** | See you Thursday at practice. You know, the guys said you were a nerd. They said you couldn't really skate. I can't wait to see their faces when you rail slide! |
| | *Exits.* |
| **JT:** | What am I going to do? I can't skate. My Mom won't even let me touch a skateboard. How the heck am I going to rail slide? What *is* a rail slide? I hang around Ricky and the guys because they're cool. Nobody knew my secret. Now I've got three days to learn everything in the world about skateboarding. I'm dead meat! |

ৰ  ৰ  ৰ

# ALMOST AWESOME
## A Scene for Three Boys

*LEE and MIXER are standing around waiting for DAN.*

**LEE:** He said he'd be here at 3:45.

**MIXER:** He'd better not be late.

**LEE:** Of course he'll be late. He's got to. It's cool.

**MIXER:** Get outta here with that.

**LEE:** And don't act like a jerk when he comes.

**MIXER:** What do you mean?

**LEE:** Just let me do the talking.

**MIXER:** I can talk if I want to.

**LEE:** No, Mixer. 'Cause you always end up starting a fight. I'm the brains, remember. Don't talk and don't act like a jerk.

**MIXER:** Listen, Lee, you're the jerk.

**LEE:** What?

**MIXER:** You act like Dan's the coolest guy on the planet.

**LEE:** He is.

**MIXER:** Oh brother!

**LEE:** He's got two Nintendos! Not one, but two. He's president of the skateboard club. President! He never wears anything but Vision Street Wear or Airwalk.

**MIXER:** Airwalk-Smairwalk! So what?

**LEE:** Shhh, here he comes.

*DAN enteres. He's totally cool.*

**DAN:** Hey dude.

**LEE:** Hey dude! (*They smack five.*)

**DAN:** Hey little dude.

**MIXER:** (*Mad.*) Who do you think you're callin' little, creep?

**LEE:** Mixer, take it easy! (*To DAN.*) So what's up?

**DAN:** Everything is righteous, my man. Totally bad. What about you, Mighty Mouth?

**MIXER:** (*Puts up his fists.*) Get him outta here, Lee?

**DAN:** Take a hyperspas man. (*To LEE.*) You got the money?

**LEE:** Yeah, right here.

*Hands DAN $5.*

**MIXER:** What the heck is that for?

**DAN:** Didn't you tell him, Lee?

**LEE:** No . . . uh . . . ah . . . maybe you'd better tell him, Dan, my man.

| DAN: | See Junior Dude, the Vision Air Side Walk Surfers and Radical Dudes of Bethesda Skateboard Club is making you guys a once in a lifetime offer. For a small small fee, we're going to let you in our club! |
| --- | --- |
| MIXER: | What? |
| DAN: | I know it's too good to be true, spud. I know, don't thank me. Even though I am the awesome president and sergeant-at-arms. Even though I am the one who told the guys in the club, "Hey give these two new geeks . . . I mean guys a break. They could be almost cool. They could be almost awesome with a little work. We can teach them." The club agreed. So now gimme 5 bucks and slap me five. |
| MIXER: | Oh, I'm gonna slap you all right. |
| DAN: | What? |
| MIXER: | (*Really angry.*) Give Lee back the 5 bucks! |
| LEE: | Mixer, what are you doing? Don't you want to join the club? |
| MIXER: | (*Shouting to DAN.*) I said give it back! |
| DAN: | Hey man, this guy's nuts. |

> *Gives LEE back the money.*

| MIXER: | We ain't payin' anybody to make us cool. We're cool enough. |
| --- | --- |
| DAN: | Hey man, that ain't a California kind of attitude. |
| MIXER: | Now, get out before I kick your . . . |

> *DAN runs out.*

| LEE: | See what you've done, Mixer? |
| --- | --- |
| MIXER: | Yeah, I've saved you again. |
| LEE: | I told you I'm the brains. |
| MIXER: | Yeah, and I'm the muscle. It's a good thing too. Now let's take that five bucks and go buy some burgers. |

❧  ❧  ❧

## SMART COOL
### A Scene for Three Girls

*JANE and CINDY work on drawings. CARRIE supervises.*

| CARRIE: | No, no. You put the cirrus clouds under that picture. Show how the wind patterns shift. |
| --- | --- |
| CINDY: | Oh yeah. O.K. I got it. |
| CARRIE: | No. No. Not "convention." The word is con*vection*. Convection carries the warm air. |
| JANE: | I always get confused. |

| | |
|---|---|
| **CARRIE:** | I don't know why. The words mean two different things. (*To CINDY.*) If you leave room here we can put in nimbus and cumulonimbus and show how temperature affects their formation. |
| **CINDY:** | This is going to be so cool. How do you know all this stuff? |
| **CARRIE:** | Reading, research, study. It's easy. You have to put your mind to it. Concentrate. |
| **JANE:** | You sure are cool. You know as much as Mrs. Taylor. |
| **CARRIE:** | If not more. |
| **JANE:** | I sure am glad I'm in your science group this time. |
| **CARRIE:** | Yeah, so I can do all the work? |
| **CINDY:** | Hey, we're working. |
| **CARRIE:** | But I come up with all the cool ideas. |
| **JANE:** | You're a genius. What can I say? |
| **CINDY:** | This is going to be an A for sure. |
| **JANE:** | Yeah, a whole week ahead of schedule. |
| **CINDY:** | Thanks to the coolest kid in the entire science class. |
| | *They all slap fives.* |
| **CARRIE:** | Now it's almost lunch time. Make sure you do a section on condensation, Jane. And Cindy you handle warm air currents. I'll do a few paragraphs on frontal activity. We'll put it together tomorrow morning. |
| **CINDY:** | Great. |
| **JANE:** | We're done. Thanks Carrie. |
| | *They start to exit.* |
| **CARRIE:** | Hey wait guys. I wanted to tell you something . . . |
| **CINDY:** | We know, don't forget the cloud chart. |
| **JANE:** | And the temperature poster. |
| **CARRIE:** | Well, yes. But that's not what I wanted to say. |
| **CINDY:** | Well what? We're going to be late for lunch. |
| **CARRIE:** | It's about lunch. |
| **JANE:** | Come on, will you? What is it? |
| **CARRIE:** | Well how come we work together all through science and you tell me how smart I am and how cool it is to work with me. Then when we get to lunch you never want to sit with me? |
| | *Pause.* |
| **JANE:** | Well . . . um . . . |
| **CINDY:** | Our table's full. |
| **CARRIE:** | Your table's full because everyone wants to sit at the cool table. |
| **JANE:** | Well sorry. We can't help it if there's no room. |
| **CINDY:** | Yup. Well we have to go now. |

| CARRIE: | No. You wait a minute. I'm tired of killing myself on this project with you guys and then getting turned away from the cool table. And don't tell me there's no room for me. I've seen you make room for Kate and Andrea and Liz and those guys. How come you can't make room for me? |
|---|---|
| JANE: | Listen, Carrie, it's just that . . . you kind of don't fit in. |
| CARRIE: | You said I was cool. |
| JANE: | Say wha? |
| CARRIE: | You did, just a while ago. |
| CINDY: | She meant that you're cool in science class. |
| CARRIE: | Right. |
| CINDY: | And that's not the same as cool in the cafeteria. |
| CARRIE: | That's ridiculous. I have a right to sit at your table. I designed the entire project. I've done most of the research. I'm practically guaranteeing that you'll get A plusses. As a matter of fact, I probably have the best grades of anybody at that entire table. |
| CINDY: | And that's exactly why you're not invited to sit there. |
| JANE: | We don't want to hear how smart you are all through lunch. |
| CINDY: | You're always showing off how much you know. Hey, you are a genius for real. But the problem is, you're always reminding us — over and over and over! |
| JANE: | When you're smart and cool you know how to relax and have fun. And how to listen to what other people have to say without showing off or putting them down. |
| CINDY: | Think about it. |

ᴥ   ᴥ   ᴥ


## IN COMMON
### A Scene for Two Girls

| KAY: | What time is it? |
|---|---|
| DELIA: | 3:15. |
| KAY: | How much longer? |
| DELIA: | It's supposed to end at 5:00. |
| KAY: | (*Sighing.*) I'm dying to get out of here. (*Pause.*) Do you know anybody? |
| DELIA: | No. Do you? |
| KAY: | No. The whole idea is ridiculous. (*Pause.*) What's your name? |
| DELIA: | Delia. |

| KAY: | I'm Kay. |
|------|----------|
| DELIA: | Hi. Now I know one person. My mother said, (*Imitating her mother.*) "If you just make one friend, I'll be happy." |
| KAY: | Well, we're not friends. I mean you know my name but we just met. So we're really not friends. |
| DELIA: | Well, I won't tell my Mom that. |
| KAY: | This is so dumb. (*Pause.*) I already have friends. |
| DELIA: | So do I. (*Pause.*) But none of them are Black. |
| KAY: | What difference does it make? That's what I want to know. (*Pause.*) What school do you go to? |
| DELIA: | Stone Valley. |
| KAY: | I go to Westfield. |
| DELIA: | I'm the only Black kid in my class. |
| KAY: | Me too, but so what. All my life my parents have told me that color does not make a difference. We're all just people. So I have white friends and oriental friends and Indian friends. I don't even think about what color they are. Now suddenly my parents are freaking out because I don't have any Black friends. |
| DELIA: | It is kind of confusing. |
| KAY: | How am I supposed to have Black friends if none are in my class? |
| DELIA: | I guess that's the reason for the party. |
| KAY: | It's still dumb. A bunch of kids thrown together just because they're Black. We don't have anything in common. We don't even know each other. |
| DELIA: | Well, now I know you. |
| KAY: | I guess. (*Pause.*) |
| DELIA: | You like Westfield? |
| KAY: | Yeah, it's great. You like Stone Valley? |
| DELIA: | Yeah. |
| KAY: | I like the friends that I have. I like them just the way they are. |
| DELIA: | Same here. (*Pause.*) Except . . . |
| KAY: | Except? |
| DELIA: | Never mind. |
| KAY: | What? |
| DELIA: | I don't know. I mean I like my friends a lot. Sometimes it's just . . . I don't know . . . a little weird . . . being . . . |
| KAY: | Being what? |
| DELIA: | Different from them. |
| KAY: | Weird like how? |
| DELIA: | Well . . . it's like . . . it's . . . never mind. |
| KAY: | No, please say it. |
| DELIA: | Like once I slept over my best friend's house. Her name is Renee and I really like her. Anyway, I took a bath there and it was summer time. She didn't |

have any cream or lotion in her house so when I came out of the tub my legs were all ashey, you know. She asked me what happened. I just said that's how I look when I'm ashey. She didn't know what that meant and kept asking me a whole bunch of questions.

**KAY:** That's funny.

**DELIA:** No it wasn't. It was a pain.

**KAY:** I mean because once I spent the night at Lisa's and the next morning my hair was smashed on one side because of how I slept. So it was standing up. And she kept saying, "Oh wow, how does it do that? Look it's standing straight up." And she kept messing around and making a big deal out of it.

**DELIA:** All my friends use hairspray, right. They put some in my hair and it was awful. My Mom freaked out.

**KAY:** My friends don't understand why my mother has to do my hair.

**DELIA:** And the day I brought a pick to school, forget it.

*They laugh.*

Then there was the time this boy Greg says to me, "I didn't know Black people like classical music. I thought they only like rap." That made me mad.

**KAY:** Once we were talking about Desmond Tutu in class and some of the kids started making fun of his name and laughing about Africa, and stuff.

**DELIA:** Yeah, stuff like that.

*Pause.*

**KAY:** It's weird, sometimes. And sometimes I get mad.

**DELIA:** You kind of don't know what to do.

**KAY:** Yeah because you can't tell your parents. My Dad would completely spaz out and call the office and speak to the principal and stuff.

**DELIA:** It's hard to tell anyone because they wouldn't understand.

**KAY:** I never told this to anybody.

**DELIA:** Now you told me.

**KAY:** (*Smiling.*) Yeah, now I told you.

❧ ❧ ❧

# RAINBOW GIRLS
## A Scene for Two Girls

**DEE:** (*Getting ready to go home.*) So thanks for the cookies and the homework.

**LYDIA:** Yuck!

**DEE:** So I'll see you at Tanya's.

68

| LYDIA: | Tanya's? |
|--------|----------|
| DEE: | You know, the party. |
| LYDIA: | What party? |
| DEE: | Come on, Lydia. The Sunshine Girls party on the 5th. |
| LYDIA: | I'm not invited to that. |
| DEE: | Huh? |
| LYDIA: | I said I wasn't invited. |
| DEE: | But all the Sunshine Girls are invited. |
| LYDIA: | Here's a news flash, Dee: yours truly was not asked to be in the Sunshine Girls. |
| DEE: | You mean you didn't try out? |
| LYDIA: | I mean I tried out and didn't get in. |
| DEE: | Get out of here. You're kidding! |
| LYDIA: | Do I look like I'm kidding? |
| DEE: | But that's crazy. |
| LYDIA: | Ask Tanya. |
| DEE: | This is stupid. |
| LYDIA: | Forget it. |
| DEE: | What reason did she give you? Why were you turned down? |
| LYDIA: | I don't want to talk about it. Forget it. I'll see you tomorrow. |
| DEE: | What did you do, belch in the middle of the interview? Spill punch on the rug? |
| LYDIA: | Look, just drop it. |
| DEE: | I'm calling Tanya. |
| LYDIA: | Don't! |
| DEE: | Well what happened? |
| LYDIA: | (*Angry.*) See this? |
| DEE: | A paper bag. |
| LYDIA: | Mean anything to you? |
| DEE: | Lots of things. Lunch, garbage, Halloween masks . . . stop me if I'm getting warm. |
| LYDIA: | (*Holds bag up to her face.*) Get it? |
| DEE: | Yeah, you've lost your mind. |
| LYDIA: | You've got a lot to learn, kid. It's the old paper bag test. Did you ever stop to think that you, Pam, Cynthia, Charlene, Marion — all of the Sunshine Girls just happen to be the same color. Did you ever think of that? |
| DEE: | No! |
| LYDIA: | That's what Sunshine Girls means. Sunshine — bright — light — yellow. |
| DEE: | Oh my God. Tell me you're kidding! |

| | |
|---|---|
| **LYDIA:** | This is for the paper bag test. They held one up to my face. The rule is that you have to be lighter than the paper bag to get in the club. I'm too dark to be a Sunshine girl. |
| **DEE:** | That's the biggest load of . . . |
| **LYDIA:** | Forget it. |
| **DEE:** | Well no way I'm staying in the club. |
| **LYDIA:** | Don't be dumb. |
| **DEE:** | But first I'm going to tell Tanya what I think of her stupid club and where she can shove her paper bag. |
| **LYDIA:** | Wait Dee. Sunshine Girls is a popular club. Think of all the great parties. All the boys. Don't give that up on account of me. |
| **DEE:** | You're my best friend. Do you think I could ever be a part of that? I'm just so mad that it happened to you. It must have really hurt your feelings. |
| **LYDIA:** | Nah. |
| **DEE:** | Yeah. |
| **LYDIA:** | Well . . . kind of. |
| **DEE:** | Why didn't you tell me? |
| **LYDIA:** | You wouldn't have understood. |
| **DEE:** | Oh no? How do you think I felt when Lee and that group of girls were trying to beat me up? |
| **LYDIA:** | Last year? I wondered what that was all about. |
| **DEE:** | Because of how I look. They thought because I'm light and have long hair that I think I'm stuck up and I show off. They didn't even know me. I ended up fighting Lee. I had to kick her butt before she'd leave me alone. And she still hates my guts. For no good reason at all. |
| **LYDIA:** | You never told me. |
| **DEE:** | You wouldn't have understood. (*Pause.*) |
| **LYDIA:** | Sometimes I wish I looked like you. Wish I had your skin color. |
| **DEE:** | Are you crazy? I wish I looked like you! Your skin is so pretty. |
| **LYDIA:** | Well so is yours! |
| **DEE:** | Well, if we're both so gorgeous, what the heck do we need the Sunshine Girls for? |
| **LYDIA:** | Yeah! We'll start our own club. The Rainbow Girls. And we'll give our own party on the 5th. |
| **DEE:** | And it will be bigger and deffer than Tanya's. |
| **LYDIA:** | So def they'll want to come themselves. |
| **DEE:** | No way, babe. Unless they come wearing those stupid paper bags over their heads! |

æ  æ  æ

# SCENES FOR MATURE GIRLS

## Introduction

As a very general rule, girls tend to mature faster than boys, and tend to be more willing to get involved in performance-oriented activities. The scenes in this section evolved from my work with mature girls in a variety of settings, including a group home school and shelter.

These scenes deal with more mature themes, including mother-daughter relationships and teen pregnancy. With mature or more advanced performers, you can get into deeper kinds of character studies and situational improvisations. "Heroine", for example, is the kind of scene that can really be used as a focus for discussion and improvisation about the monumental responsibilities of being a teen mother. The scene can be a real learning experience for teen boys as well. They too have much to learn about the tremendous responsibilities involved with fathering a child.

Should you find that you have an all-girl cast and you wish to put together a program, consider also borrowing some of the scenes from *The Only One Who Knows* that are easily adaptable for female performers.


## LADY

NINA:  My mother raised me to be a lady. Honest! When I was a little girl, I wore my hair in two long braids with bows on the ends. I wore pretty white pumps and dresses with big fluffy petticoats. And where did that get me? "Don't fight! Ladies don't fight!" my mother screams at me. What kind of world are you living in, Ma? I'm getting slaughtered out here. I'm getting tripped and smacked and beaten up out here. Who's going to defend me if I don't defend myself? If you don't want me to fight, you'd better move me out of this neighborhood. You'd better find me another school. You'd better find me some magic words to keep these animals off of me. I don't want to fight. I want to be a lady more than anything else in this world. But I've got to survive first!

ख़   ख़   ख़


## HEROINE
### A Scene for Two Girls

LIZ:  Where's Shanice, Dolores, Cookie and them?

VONNIE: In school. I skipped 3rd period. Didn't they come by?

LIZ:  No. Nobody came. I haven't seen anyone since I've been home.

VONNIE: Well, I'm here now.

LIZ:  (*Sarcastic.*) Terrific.

71

| | |
|---|---|
| **VONNIE:** | You did that great just now. |
| **LIZ:** | I only gave her a bottle. |
| **VONNIE:** | Yeah, but you look like a real mommy doing it. She's so cute. |
| **LIZ:** | Shut up or she'll wake up again. |

*Pause.*

| | |
|---|---|
| **VONNIE:** | You look great. |
| **LIZ:** | Do not. |
| **VONNIE:** | Do so. |
| **LIZ:** | I'm fat and ugly. |
| **VONNIE:** | No you're not. |
| **LIZ:** | My stomach looks like an an elephant's — all rolling and wrinkly. It's disgusting. |
| **VONNIE:** | It'll go back. |
| **LIZ:** | Not like before. |
| **VONNIE:** | You'll be looking as sharp as ever. Just you wait. |
| **LIZ:** | Some girls just stay fat for the rest of their lives. |
| **VONNIE:** | Not you, Liz. You're beautiful, I mean it. And Tina is so cute. She's just like a sweet little baby doll. |
| **LIZ:** | A baby doll that does nothing but cry. |
| **VONNIE:** | She's asleep now. |
| **LIZ:** | 24 hours a day, round the clock and all through the night — cry, suck and mess in her diaper. That's all she does. |
| **VONNIE:** | What do you do? |
| **LIZ:** | What? |
| **VONNIE:** | When she makes a mess in her diaper? |
| **LIZ:** | What the heck do you think, Vonnie? I clean it up. |
| **VONNIE:** | Is it awful? |
| **LIZ:** | Well, what do you think? |
| **VONNIE:** | Oh. |
| **LIZ:** | I ain't got time for stupid questions. I ain't hardly got time to shower and brush my teeth and comb my hair before she starts bawling again. |
| **VONNIE:** | You going to come back to school? |
| **LIZ:** | And what am I supposed to do with Tina, stuff her in my three-ring binder? |
| **VONNIE:** | Won't your mother keep her? |
| **LIZ:** | Mama has to work. Besides, she ain't keeping the baby. She told me that. Said it's *my* baby. *My* responsibility. So I have to do everything. |
| **VONNIE:** | She mad at you? |
| **LIZ:** | Not so much anymore. She likes to hold Tina and all that. But said she's raised her own kids, now I gotta raise mine. |

| VONNIE: | Well that's good, in a way. She won't interfere. You'll have more independence. |
|---|---|

*LIZ suddenly starts to cry.*

| LIZ: | Why don't you just get out of here! |
|---|---|
| VONNIE: | Liz, what's wrong? Don't cry. Please. |
| LIZ: | Get out! |
| VONNIE: | What did I say? |
| LIZ: | (*Angry.*) Independence! Can't you see I'm in jail here? I'm choking to death in this place. I can't go any place. I can't do anything for the rest of my life. I wish I had never done it. I wish she was never born. I want my life back the way it was! |
| VONNIE: | (*Patting her.*) Please don't cry. (*Hands her a tissue.*) I don't know what to say. |
| LIZ: | Didn't ask you to say anything. You can just go on back to 3rd period and tell everybody what a mess I am. |
| VONNIE: | I wouldn't do that. |
| LIZ: | That's why you came wasn't it? Shanice, Dolores, Cookie and them ain't even called. Supposed to be my best friends. And you here snooping around asking dumb questions and getting me all upset so you can run on back to school and tell everybody how bad off I am. I guess now that I'm gone you can stand a chance with the guys, huh? You wait til I'm fat and ugly cause that's the only way you'd ever stand a chance. |
| VONNIE: | A chance to end up like you? |

*Pause.*

I didn't mean to say that.

| LIZ: | Yes you did. |
|---|---|
| VONNIE: | You made me mad. I came all the way over here and you haven't even said thanks — not one nice word to me since I got here. I'm not Shanice or Dolores or Cookie so I guess you don't even think of me as a friend, huh? Well then I must be as stupid as you say I am. |
| LIZ: | You know you're not stupid. |
| VONNIE: | Oh, yes I am. Because you've always been a heroine for me. |
| LIZ: | Say what? |
| VONNIE: | Heroine. Not the drug, dummy. A hero — a female hero. |
| LIZ: | Yeah, right. |
| VONNIE: | I'm not beautiful or popular. The guys don't hang around me and stuff. Not like with you. So I always kind of . . . |
| LIZ: | Kind of what? |
| VONNIE: | Looked up to you. You were like my . . . |
| LIZ: | What? |
| VONNIE: | It sounds stupid. (*Pause.*) Like my idol or something . . . |
| LIZ: | And now? |
| VONNIE: | And now . . . I thought . . . maybe? |

| | |
|---|---|
| **LIZ:** | What? |
| **VONNIE:** | Maybe I could be a friend. I know I couldn't be like Dolores or Cookie. But I could sit here with Tina while you take a shower. Maybe I could sit here if you want to take a walk. But I have to be back for 5th period. |
| **LIZ:** | (*Pause.*) I'm sorry. |
| **VONNIE:** | Why? |
| **LIZ:** | Because I'm not your heroine any more. |
| **VONNIE:** | Maybe a friend is better. |
| **LIZ:** | (*Hugging VONNIE.*) Thanks. |

❧   ❧   ❧

# ANNIE-MATIC

**ANNIE:** Sometimes I lay very still and smash things with my mind. My windows with the white lace ruffled curtains. Pow! The mirror on my dresser with pictures of Dad and Malcolm- Jamal Warner stuck down into the frame. Crash — tinkle, tinkle, tinkle! Charlene's second runner up trophy from the Miss Black Teenage Northern Maryland Pageant — oooh that's delicious. I can hear it. KABAM! Shards and slivers of glass up to the ceiling. Down to the carpet. I smash things with my mind because I am a peaceful person. Miss Sobel wrote a word on my personal development report . . . (*She spells it.*) e-n-i-g- m-a-t-i-c. Enigmatic. I like that. I call it Annie-matic. Because my name's Annie and I'm on automatic all the time. I am so damn nice to everybody. Automatically, all the time. My sister Charlene comes home with her boyfriend Horrible Horace, and they want to study up here in OUR room. Of course then OUR room becomes HER room.

*Imitating Charlene.*

"Annie be a sugar pie and go on in the living room. Horace and I need to study." Sure. And I'm the Queen of Sheba. Of course I could be because I read where the Queen of Sheba was a Black woman. Woman? Yes, I would describe myself as a woman. I'm certainly more mature than Charlene. But when she asks me to leave, do I say "Heck no!"? Do I stand up for my room rights?

No. I'm Annie-matic on the sofa watching Happy Days. I'm solid, dependable Annie-matic. And I smash things in my mind because I wouldn't actually pick something up and break it. You feel terrible when you smash something. You feel even worse if it's done to you. Like when I overheard Stephanie and Allison talking about Black people in the girl's bathroom last year, before I changed schools. That's how it felt. My heart going Crash, tinkle, tinkle, tinkle, like Charlene's trophy. You know, I finally looked up enigmatic in the dictionary. I like to throw big words around like that to drive Charlene crazy. "Mysterious," it said. I was surprised. I wonder if Miss Sobel knows that sometimes I like to lay real still and smash things with my mind. KABAM! Horrible Horace's brand new Christian Dior frames with tinted lenses smashed to powdered glass.

74

# ENRICHMENT

*The sleeping figure of Maryann's Mom lies on the bed with her back to the audience. She is still throughout. On a table nearby are an empty liquor bottle and a glass. MARYANN covers her Mom.*

**MARYANN:** I guess I hurt your feelings. I didn't mean to. Well, maybe I did. You asked me and I told you the truth. Why do you ask me those dumb questions anyway. I know (*Imitating counselor.*) "Enrichment." That counselor doesn't know a damn thing about me. Why do you believe all that garbage? (*Imitating counselor.*) "Enrichment, Mrs. Myers. Enrichment builds a quality relationship." We had one. You and me, back then. In the days when you still wore that flannel nightgown with the red flowers on it. When I was young enough to crawl into your bed, and fall asleep while you read your law books and ate slices of American cheese. Everytime I smell Kraft American singles, I think of that wonderful time. So, you asked me, so I told you. No I don't want to be like you. I don't want to be a lawyer or a single parent or an alcoholic. Well, you always said I got my fast mouth from you. Straight talk. (*Imitating counselor.*) "Enrichment, Maryann. Be honest with your mother." Well, you know what? Honestly? Once I wanted to be like you so much I hated you. Back then when I wore your pearl earrings to school and lost one. (*Laughs.*) You slapped me so hard. I was a rotten brat. But I wanted to look like you and talk like you and walk the way you did with your briefcase. (*Imitating Mother.*) Maryann, meet me at the dentist's and then we'll go for soup at O'Rooney's. Soup was all I could eat after those braces. Oh, Mom. It had nothing to do with the divorce. It was you. (*Indicating bottle.*) This is gonna look just great on you in court tomorrow. Listen, I'm sorry I said what I said, but when you start drinking before a big case, well . . . you broke a rule. (*Angry.*) So don't say a damn thing about what time I come home or what I wear or who the hell I go out with! If you break your rules, I break mine. You asked me and I told you. I don't want to be like you. Not the way you are now. I want to be that little fuzzy-headed lady in the red flowered nighty curled up in the bed eating American cheese.

*Kisses her sleeping Mom.*

See you tomorrow.

☙  ☙  ☙

# NO JUSTICE

**ELLIE:** What am I, a piece of the wall? Who am I, the invisible woman? When I walk down the street with her, nobody even sees me. People actually walk all over me trying to get close to her. If I drop a book, people step on it and keep on going. If she drops a book, sixteen hands catch it before it even hits the ground. What the heck does she have that I don't have? I've got brains — she's got feathers. I'm sensitive — she's got a heart of concrete. I'm good-looking — she's a doggone cover girl, beauty queen, knock-out! That's all they see. That's all they care about. I'd hate her guts if she wasn't my best friend. There's just no justice!

# IF I COULD BE YOU
## A Scene for Mother and Daughter

| | |
|---|---|
| **CLAIRE:** | Come on. Sit down. |
| **LIZZIE:** | What? I'm in the middle of my homework. |
| **CLAIRE:** | Oh? Since when is that important? |
| **LIZZIE:** | I want to finish. There's a party. You said I could go. Remember? |
| **CLAIRE:** | I want to talk to you. |
| **LIZZIE:** | What? |
| **CLAIRE:** | Sit down. |
| **LIZZIE:** | (*Sitting.*) What? |
| **CLAIRE:** | I got a call from Mr. Mosby today. |

> *Pause.*

| | |
|---|---|
| **LIZZIE:** | So? |
| **CLAIRE:** | Where have you been going while the rest of your classmates learn English Composition? |
| **LIZZIE:** | What? |
| **CLAIRE:** | I've got all evening. If you want to play games, I've got plenty of time. |
| **LIZZIE:** | Mom. |
| **CLAIRE:** | Then answer my question. |
| **LIZZIE:** | What? (*Pause.*) You wanna know if I went some place? |
| **CLAIRE:** | You got it. |
| **LIZZIE:** | Yeah, I did. |
| **CLAIRE:** | Yes? |
| **LIZZIE:** | What? |
| **CLAIRE:** | If you say "what" one more time, you're grounded for two weeks. |
| **LIZZIE:** | Wha . . . (*Catches herself.*) Look, Mom, I didn't do anything bad. |
| **CLAIRE:** | You've missed English class five times in a row. I want to know where you were. |
| **LIZZIE:** | I didn't feel good. I went to the nurse. |
| **CLAIRE:** | I'll cut off your phone privileges one night for every lie you tell me, Lizzie. I'm not fooling around with you. |
| **LIZZIE:** | God, I feel like I'm at the Inquisition or something. |
| **CLAIRE:** | Well, at least you've been in History class. Now where have you been for the last five Wednesdays at 12:13? |
| **LIZZIE:** | I've been going . . . out. |
| **CLAIRE:** | Out of the school? |
| **LIZZIE:** | Yes. |
| **CLAIRE:** | It is my understanding that that's against school rules. |

| | |
|---|---|
| **LIZZIE:** | (*Standing.*) Yeah, well I won't do it anymore, O.K.? |
| **CLAIRE:** | I'm not finished. (*Pause.*) I said I'm not finished. (*LIZZIE sits.*) Where do you go? |
| **LIZZIE:** | When? |
| **CLAIRE:** | It's as if you want me to punish you. You're pushing me to do it. So then you can sulk and moan around the house and call your father to tell him how I mistreat you. |
| **LIZZIE:** | I do not. |
| **CLAIRE:** | Well stop being a smart mouth. I want to know where you went, why, with whom, and what the heck you did. |
| **LIZZIE:** | You think you're angry now? Wait til I tell you! |
| **CLAIRE:** | Right, you're in for the evening. No party. |
| **LIZZIE:** | Damn you. |
| **CLAIRE:** | I'll slap your face. |
| **LIZZIE:** | (*Shouting.*) I was with Dad. I went to see Dad. O.K.? |
| **CLAIRE:** | I don't believe you. |
| **LIZZIE:** | I knew you wouldn't. O.K., you want me to tell you that I went out on the back of Bret's motorcycle, drinking beer and mugging old ladies? O.K., that's what I did. Whatever you want to believe. |
| **CLAIRE:** | I'll know if you're lying. I'll call your father. |
| **LIZZIE:** | That would be a miracle. |
| | *Pause.* |
| **CLAIRE:** | You skipped English to see your father? |
| **LIZZIE:** | I told you. (*Pause.*) He had a bunch of meetings at this building near school. I met him at the coffee shop. |
| **CLAIRE:** | Typical of him to take you out of English for his own selfish reasons. |
| **LIZZIE:** | So what now? You gonna keep me in for the rest of my life? Rip my phone out of the wall? |
| **CLAIRE:** | Hush. |
| **LIZZIE:** | Can I go? |
| | *Pause.* |
| **CLAIRE:** | What did you do? |
| **LIZZIE:** | What do you mean? Oh, is it O.K. to say "what" now? |
| **CLAIRE:** | You and your father? What did you do? |
| **LIZZIE:** | Different stuff. |
| **CLAIRE:** | Like what? |
| **LIZZIE:** | We talked. |
| **CLAIRE:** | About me, I suppose. |
| **LIZZIE:** | Oh, boy, here we go. |
| **CLAIRE:** | About how badly I treat you? How we don't have any money? |

| | |
|---|---|
| **LIZZIE:** | Think what you want to think. Whatever I tell you you're going to think what you want to think. |
| **CLAIRE:** | Well, it's going to stop. Do you hear me? I want you in class, in school, where you belong. |
| **LIZZIE:** | Right. Can I go now? |
| **CLAIRE:** | I suppose you had company. |
| **LIZZIE:** | What? |
| **CLAIRE:** | A cozy threesome. |
| **LIZZIE:** | Right. Me, Dad and the waitress. |
| **CLAIRE:** | Not what's-her-name? |
| **LIZZIE:** | Come on, Mom. |
| **CLAIRE:** | Well, I want it to stop. You're in school all day Wednesday and every single day. I don't ever want to hear that you're skipping classes for any reason. Particularly not to hang out at coffee shops. |
| **LIZZIE:** | Particularly not with my father. |
| **CLAIRE:** | Nor his little girlfriend. |
| **LIZZIE:** | I need to talk to him sometimes. I need him too, you know. |
| **CLAIRE:** | Well, he can come on the weekends, like he's supposed to. |
| **LIZZIE:** | He's been away. You can't schedule him and boss him around like you do to me. The divorce means he's free. (*Pause.*) |
| **CLAIRE:** | In school, got it? |
| **LIZZIE:** | Yeah. Can I go now? (*Pause.*) Can I go? (*Pause.*) |
| **CLAIRE:** | I'll talk to him. See if I can . . . be more flexible . . . about the visits. I'll see. |
| **LIZZIE:** | Yeah. |

*Stands up. Starts to exit, but stops. Thinks, then speaks.*

He won't bring her. He knows I'm not ready for that. But he showed me her picture.

| | |
|---|---|
| **CLAIRE:** | Yeah? |
| **LIZZIE:** | Her teeth are funny. |

*Pause.*

| | |
|---|---|
| **CLAIRE:** | (*Smiling.*) Thanks. |

*They freeze and come downstage.*

| | |
|---|---|
| **LIZZIE:** | If you could be me, Mom . . . |
| **CLAIRE:** | If I could be you? |
| **LIZZIE:** | You'd be quite amazed by an insider's view<br>You'd discover so much that you never knew<br>If you could be me, Mom. |
| **CLAIRE:** | Well, then, I'll be you. |

*She fixes her hair like Lizzie's and borrows an article of Lizzie's clothing.*

|  | If you could be me, dear. |
| **LIZZIE:** | If I could be you? |
| **CLAIRE:** | You'd have to do all that a mother would do. |
|  | You'd view the whole world and your feelings anew. |
|  | If you could be me, dear. |
| **LIZZIE:** | Well then, I'll be you. |

*She fixes her hair like Claire's and borrows a piece of Claire's clothing. The scene starts again — same movements but with the roles reversed. CLAIRE plays LIZZIE the daughter, LIZZIE plays CLAIRE, the mother.*

| **CLAIRE:** | Sweetie, come here for a minute. |
| **LIZZIE:** | O.K. Mom, what's up? |
| **CLAIRE:** | I want to ask you a question. It's not because I'm checking up on you. You know I trust you. |
| **LIZZIE:** | Anything Mom. Ask away. I don't hide anything from you. |
| **CLAIRE:** | O.K. Mr. Mosby says you've missed five English Comp classes. Is that true? |
| **LIZZIE:** | Yes, Mom. I meant to tell you. I'm sorry. |
| **CLAIRE:** | I know you had a good reason, Lizzie. You don't have to tell me if you don't want to. |
| **LIZZIE:** | I want to, Mom. I don't keep secrets from you. I met Daddy in a coffee shop near school. I hope you're not mad. I know I should have asked permission first. |
| **CLAIRE:** | I'm so happy you and he got a chance to spend some time together. I know you miss him. |
| **LIZZIE:** | I guess I need to talk to him more often. I wish he'd come on the weekends, like he promised. |
| **CLAIRE:** | Well I know his schedule's busy. Tell you what, I'll give him a call right now and see if we can't arrange some visits during the week. That will be easier on both of you. |
| **LIZZIE:** | I don't want him to bring his new girlfriend. |
| **CLAIRE:** | Lizzie, you have nothing to worry about. I'm sure she's very nice. Beside she will never come between you and me. Even if she and Dad get married, I'll always be your real Mom. We'll always be close. |
| **LIZZIE:** | You're right, Mom. I love you so much. And she's so completely horrible looking! |

*Freeze. Then LIZZIE and CLAIRE go back to the way they were before. They give back each other's clothing.*

| **LIZZIE:** | If I could be you . . . |
| **CLAIRE:** | If I could be you . . . |
| **TOGETHER:** | . . . AND YOU COULD BE ME. |

🐦 🐦 🐦

# THE ONLY ONE WHO KNOWS

## Introduction

It is extremely rare to get a cast comprised completely of adolescent male performers. Boys, as a very general rule, will opt for sports over performance activities if given a choice.

In the case of developing this script, however, the boys did not have a choice. The project was a mandatory part of an English assignment at a group home school in Montgomery County. The script was developed through discussions and workshop activities.

The cast was racially mixed, and I took this opportunity to explore some racial issues in the scene, "Waiting." I also explored the color/status issue among black youth in the scene "Beautiful." Other scenes and monologues deal with universal themes.

We performed this piece in the living room of the dormintory, which put the boys very close to the audience and give it an incredible realism. We used the furniture at hand. Our only props were a comic book in the scene, "Beautiful" and a duffle bag in the scene, "Leaving."

The music we used in the production were currently popular hits. Ask your performers for their input on what music is current that will highlight the themes of the pieces.

## Scenes and Monologues

# THE ONLY ONE WHO KNOWS

| | |
|---|---|
| **DOMINIC:** | Don't judge before you've listened. |
| **COOL BREEZE:** | Don't speak before you've heard. |
| **NIPSY:** | You may think you know me, |
| **NATHANIEL:** | But you don't just take my word. |
| **OMAR:** | Don't laugh before the punchline, |
| **MUSTAPHA:** | Don't shed a single tear. |
| **JESSIE:** | Keep eyes and minds wide open |
| **ZEB:** | So that your heart can hear. |
| **BUTCH:** | Don't think that you can tell |
| **DE LEON:** | By looking at my clothes |
| **SLIM:** | What I feel deep inside myself |
| **ALL:** | I'm the only one who knows —<br>I'm the only one who knows. |

# EXPLORER

**DE LEON:** De Leon. Yeah, you heard right. That's my first name. When I was little, I hated it. People called me "Da Lion" or "Dandelion." After awhile I didn't even bother to correct them. Whatever they wanted to call me, fine. I was mad at my mother for naming me that anyway. Then one day the teacher says, "We're going to study the namesake of one of your classmates today." I was only half listening and I didn't know what namesake meant. Then she hands out this book — *The Travels of Ponce de Leon*. De Leon — hey, that's me. Now check this out. He was an explorer, and wasn't I the first on my block to ride my bike over the 5th Street Hill? He was a nobleman, and isn't everyone always talking about how I walk around with an attitude? He was a soldier. I've made my point! From that day on, I forgave my mother and I correct anybody who doesn't say it right. De Leon. It fits!

ɞ  ɞ  ɞ

# COOL BREEZE

**COOL BREEZE:** I don't care what it says on that paper, I'm telling you. My name is Cool Breeze. That's my name. Because you can't catch me. You can't hold me. I'm that sweet, refreshing moment that you wish would stay. But I'm gone. Yes it *is* my real name, because I gave it to myself. Nobody else ever knew me long enough or well enough to give me a name. Birthdate? August 5, 1987. That's right. That's the day I came stumbling out of the darkness into the real world — eyes open and screaming my lungs out. If you're flat on your belly on the floor of life, you can do one of two things — wait til somebody steps on you or get up and start running. I'm master of the chase. I'm Cool Breeze. A quick smile and I'm gone. An echo of laughter and — I'm out of here!

&a &a &a

# BEAUTIFUL

**SLIM:** Man, she's beautiful!

**NIPSY:** Uh huh.

**SLIM:** She's fine.

**NIPSY:** Uh huh.

**SLIM:** She's like a dream.

**NIPSY:** Right.

**SLIM:** When I look at her, bombs go off in my head.

**NIPSY:** Oh man, she ain't that fine.

**SLIM:** Are you crazy? I've never seen a girl as fine as she is.

**NIPSY:** O.K.

**SLIM:** Have you?

**NIPSY:** What?

**SLIM:** Have you ever seen a girl that beautiful?

**NIPSY:** I don't know.

**SLIM:** Don't know. Either you have or you haven't. (*Pause.*) Well?

**NIPSY:** Why don't you leave me alone about this?

**SLIM:** I want to know.

**NIPSY:** What? Why do you keep bothering me?

**SLIM:** She is incredible.

**NIPSY:** Man, will you shut up.

| SLIM: | You jealous, brother? You jealous because she spoke to me and not you? |
|---|---|
| NIPSY: | Spoke to you? All she did was ask you which train goes to Metro Center. |
| SLIM: | Yeah, but HOW did she ask me? |
| NIPSY: | You're being ridiculous. |
| SLIM: | You saw that sparkle in her eyes. |
| NIPSY: | That was the reflection of the headlights from the oncoming train. |
| SLIM: | And she smiled. |
| NIPSY: | Boy, you need to take a rest. |
| SLIM: | I should have asked her for her phone number. |
| NIPSY: | Yeah, and ended this nonsense once and for all. |
| SLIM: | What do you mean? |
| NIPSY: | Now you know she wouldn't give you her phone number. |
| SLIM: | Bet she would. |
| NIPSY: | You're sick. |
| SLIM: | Why not? Why wouldn't she? She could have asked five other people on the platform. That old lady or that college guy. She could have asked them about the train. She could have asked you. But she asked me. |
| NIPSY: | Directions for the Metro. That's all. |
| SLIM: | I could have called her if I had gotten her number. I could have gone by her house to pick her up and take her out some place. |
| NIPSY: | Like where? |
| SLIM: | The ballet. A girl like that would like ballet. |
| NIPSY: | A girl like that would say, "Fool are you crazy? Now stop bothering me. Get off my phone and stop wasting my time!" Click. |
| SLIM: | Did you see her, man? Skin like coffee with a whole lot of cream. Long pretty hair just hanging down. Did you see her eyes, man? They were green! |
| NIPSY: | Man, shut up! You always talking about some red bone. You forgotten Bernita already? How she tore you up and stomped on your heart. What about Cynthia? Didn't she make a fool of you too? |
| SLIM: | They were different. |
| NIPSY: | You're hung up on that look, man. That's all you care about. She could have the soul of The Alien, the temper of Conan the Barbarian, and the heart of The Terminator. But all you see is light skin and light eyes. |
| SLIM: | It's pretty. |
| NIPSY: | I'm telling you, man, you'd better find somebody you like. A girl who's nice. |
| SLIM: | How do you know *she's* not nice? |
| NIPSY: | Seemed to me that when you smiled at her, she turned to ice. Seemed to me, and I was watching pretty carefully, like she put her nose up in the air and sat way down at the other end of the platform on purpose. Seems to me like you're living in some kind of dream world. That's why you're always getting hurt. I've seen you pass up lots of girls who really like you, just because they weren't light enough. |

| | |
|---|---|
| **SLIM:** | So? |
| **NIPSY:** | It's like you're saying there's something wrong with being dark. Like a dark girl is ugly or something. |
| **SLIM:** | Oh, man . . . you're just being . . . |
| **NIPSY:** | And I'm dark. And so are all my sisters. So what are you saying? |
| **SLIM:** | I haven't said anything about your sisters. |
| **NIPSY:** | And you'd better not. Ever! |
| | *He exits.* |
| **SLIM:** | Say, man. What's your problem? |

ᕷ ᕷ ᕷ


## SUMMER JOB

| | |
|---|---|
| **ZEB:** | I got a summer job at a computer place last year. Assistant to the Guard and General Mail Person. Anyway, it paid more than laying around my house looking at TV. They made me dress business style because I had to go in and out of the front office. My Uncle got me the job and he took me to buy some clothes. Man, I had never thought about wearing stuff like that. I thought wing tips were part of the Space Shuttle. The first day, everyone's checking me out. I'm checking everybody else out. They act like I'm going to sneak the Xerox machine out under my suit. But things got better. In fact, I moved up to the point where they had me answering phones on the secretary's break. "Good Morning, Century Computers!" I had to check myself out. Talking like somebody else, dressing like somebody else. But see, I found out I can do it if I want to. If I have to. I'll do it if that's what it takes to get up there. 'Cause I'm heading up there., You heard it here first! |

ᕷ ᕷ ᕷ


## THE CLOCK

| | |
|---|---|
| **ZEB:** | Clock keeps ticking on the wall. |
| **DOMINIC:** | Saying, "Man, get on the ball!" |
| **BUTCH:** | On a digital, the time goes quick. |
| **COOL B.:** | Better get with it, get on the stick. |
| **DE LEON:** | You may stumble, you may fall |
| **JESSIE:** | You may try to duck and stall. |
| **OMAR:** | Keep putting off until tomorrow, |

84

| | |
|---|---|
| **NIPSY:** | You're just in for grief and sorrow. |
| **SLIM:** | Lay back, take your ease and chill, |
| **NATHAN:** | But time keeps rollin' down the hill. |
| **MUSTAPHA:** | I'll tell you this, whatever you do. |
| **ALL:** | Don't let time run out on you. |
| | Don't let time run out on you. |

ð   ð   ð

# WHO DO YOU THINK YOU ARE?

**MUSTAPHA:** "Who do you think you are?" "Just who do you think you are?" I have a teacher who says that to me all the time. I just laugh. Of course she is angry to start and when I laugh she gets even angrier. "Who do you think you are?" If she keeps asking, one of these days, I'm going to tell her. I think I am someone great, because I have wonderful dreams. I think I am an artist because I have the power to change the universe. I think I have more talent and energy in my little finger than you'll see in your entire life time. Because when she says, "Who do you think you are?" she really means, "You are nothing." So I just laugh. Because the day I start believing that, I'm dead.

ð   ð   ð

# WAITING

*BUTCH stands waiting at a bus stop. DOMINIC stands on the other side of the stage. They pace. They look at each other furtively.*

| | |
|---|---|
| **DOM:** | Butch? |
| **BUTCH:** | Yeah? |
| **DOM:** | Hey, Butch! I thought it might be you. |
| **BUTCH:** | (*Chuckles.*) Yeah, it's me. |
| **DOM:** | You remember me? Dominic? I moved a few years ago. We were on the same football team and everything. |
| **BUTCH:** | I remember you. |
| **DOM:** | So, how're you doing? |
| **BUTCH:** | Good. |
| **DOM:** | Great. (*Pause.*) So you live around here? |
| **BUTCH:** | I was visiting somebody. |

*Pause.*

This where you live?

DOM: Near here.

BUTCH: Where do you go now?

DOM: Burton. (*Pause.*) So how are the other guys at Carter? Zach, Billy, Manny?

BUTCH: Fine.

DOM: You remember that guy with red hair and freckles?

BUTCH: Paul?

DOM: Paul right. Tell them all I said hello. We had good times on the team.

BUTCH: How long were you standing over there?

DOM: I don't know.

BUTCH: 45 minutes. I spotted you as soon as I saw you. When did you see me?

DOM: When I walked up here. You looked familiar from over there.

BUTCH: (*Laughs.*) You saw me Dom. And you knew me right away. What's all that "Hey remember me" crap? You know me, I know you. And we spotted each other right away 45 minutes ago. We've been standing here pretending not to know each other for the last 45 minutes.

DOM: I didn't see you.

BUTCH: You didn't want to see me. You were standing in the middle of all your new friends.

DOM: I just didn't see you. (*Pause.*) Sometimes you think you see somebody you know and it isn't.

BUTCH: But this time, it is.

*Pause.*

So I guess you didn't want your new friends to know.

DOM: Come on, Butch.

BUTCH: Dom, you ate dinner at my house every Friday night. I ate dinner at yours every Saturday. I went fishing with you and your cousins in Pennsylvania. We were best friends. And you're gonna ask if I remember you?

DOM: I wasn't sure.

*Pause.*

They wouldn't have understood. It wouldn't have been cool.

BUTCH: Yeah, I know.

*Pause.*

DOM: Put yourself in my place. You're with a bunch of white guys. You see me. You gonna bring them all over to say hi? You gonna tell them, "I'd like you to meet this black guy who was like a brother to me." (*Pause.*) Would you have done that?

BUTCH: I don't know.

DOM: The hell you don't. (*Pause.*)

| BUTCH: | It's stupid. It shouldn't be like that. |
|---|---|
| DOM: | I didn't make the rules. |
| BUTCH: | Neither did I. |
| DOM: | No, but your Daddy did. |
| BUTCH: | My Daddy works in a candy store, Dom. You know that. He doesn't even make the rules for himself, much less anybody else. |
| DOM: | You know what I mean. |
| BUTCH: | Yeah, but my Dad's got enough problems. He's not taking the rap for slavery too. |
| DOM: | So I'm supposed to? |
| | *Pause.* |
| BUTCH: | It's messed up. |
| DOM: | I know. (*Pause.*) My friends would have given you and me a lot of hassles. I waited until they left. I wanted to say hello. |
| BUTCH: | Hello. |
| DOM: | Hello and goodbye. I've got to get home. Finals. |
| BUTCH: | Right. |
| DOM: | Say hello to your Mom. |
| BUTCH: | Say hello to yours too. |
| DOM: | Well, I'll see you. |
| | *They shake. DOM walks away.* |
| BUTCH: | (*To himself.*) I don't think so. |

꙳   ꙳   ꙳

## THE BIG "A"

NATHANIEL: "You'd better." "You should." "You have to." It's the voice of the Big A. I hear that and I go nuts. I'm a sane, level-headed guy. I can be responsible, even. Left on my own, I usually come up with the right solutions and do the right thing. JUST DON'T TELL ME WHAT TO DO! Yeah, I make mistakes. Some of them were serious and I'm paying for them now. But that's the point: *I* pay, not you. Give me advice, I try to listen. I might even do what you suggest once in a while. Just don't come at me with that "Do what I tell you to do" 'cause I'll turn around and do the opposite to get back at you — even if it hurts me. See, from the adults I know, they're just as scared and confused as we are. But they can cover it up with authority — the Big A. So if you want to talk to me, better come at me straight. Leave the Big A at the door. Just talk to me.

## LEAVING

| | |
|---|---|
| **JESSE:** | That everything? |
| **OMAR:** | Yeah. |
| **JESSIE:** | You got your stuff out of the bathroom? |
| **OMAR:** | Yeah. |
| **JESSIE:** | You got your bus ticket? |
| **OMAR:** | What are you, my mother? |
| **JESSIE:** | Just wanted to make sure you got everything. Because I don't know your address and if you left something I wouldn't know how to get it to you. |
| **OMAR:** | I've got everything. |
| **JESSIE:** | I guess they'd just put it in the lost and found or something. |
| **OMAR:** | It's all here. |
| **JESSIE:** | And somebody would probably steal it out of the lost and found and you'd never see it. |
| **OMAR:** | I said I've got everything. |
| | *Pause.* |
| **JESSIE:** | So what time are you leaving? |
| **OMAR:** | A few minutes. |
| **JESSIE:** | So, you're going to be with your Uncle? |
| **OMAR:** | Yeah. |
| **JESSIE:** | Greg said you were going to Philly. |
| **OMAR:** | I didn't tell Greg that. |
| **JESSIE:** | Oh. He must have gotten mixed up then. (*Pause.*) Where did you say you were going? |
| **OMAR:** | I didn't say. |
| **JESSIE:** | Oh. (*Pause.*) So where? |
| **OMAR:** | Where what? |
| **JESSIE:** | Where will you be? You know, like if you leave something and they want to send it to you? |
| **OMAR:** | I told you, man. I have everything here in this bag. And if I leave something, you can have it. Just take it. I don't want it. As a matter of fact, if I had the money, I'd leave this whole bag. Shirts, pants, pajamas, toothbrush, everything. They remind me of this place. All I want to do is forget everything. Forget I was ever here and start over. Like putting an eraser on the blackboard and wiping it all off. |
| **JESSIE:** | So if anything's left, I can have it? |

88

| | |
|---|---|
| **OMAR:** | (*Angry.*) I didn't leave anything! |
| | *JESSIE turns to walk out.* |
| | Yo', where are you going? |
| **JESSIE:** | It's late. I've got to be somewhere. |
| **OMAR:** | Where? Where do you have to be? You have an appointment at the White House? |
| | *JESSIE starts to walk out again. OMAR calls him.* |
| | I thought you were going to wait. |
| **JESSIE:** | Why? |
| **OMAR:** | Cab's gonna be here any minute. |
| **JESSIE:** | I'm not going to watch you get into the cab. You want to erase everything? So do I. |
| **OMAR:** | Hey, I just meant . . . |
| **JESSIE:** | I got eyes. You ain't nothing to me. Not a friend. Not a guy I even knew. That's cool. I'm not begging you for anything. |
| **OMAR:** | I meant that I . . . |
| **JESSIE:** | I know what you meant. What did you think I was going to do? Write and ask you for money? Show up at your Uncle's house and embarrass you? |
| **OMAR:** | Come on, man. |
| **JESSIE:** | Anything you leave here is going in the garbage. |
| **OMAR:** | Here! I wrote this out last night. It has your name on it. There's a letter inside with my new address and phone number. Don't open it now and don't tell anybody you know where I am. I've seen other guys leave and it gets strange. Saying goodbye gets weird. I just kind of wanted to slip away and not make a big deal. |
| **JESSIE:** | Yeah. |
| **OMAR:** | I didn't want to get dumb about this. |
| **JESSIE:** | Why not? You're dumb about everything else. |
| | *They laugh briefly.* |
| **OMAR:** | So, take it easy. |
| **JESSIE:** | You too, man. |
| | *Pause.* |
| | You scared? |
| **OMAR:** | Out of my mind. |
| **JESSIE:** | Be cool. |
| **OMAR:** | Right. |
| | *They shake. JESSIE exits.* |

# THE PROMISE

**BUTCH:**    When I was young it seems there was
so much I did not know.

**DE LEON:**    When I was young things came to me
all tied up in a bow.

**JESSIE:**    No holes, no rips, no hanging ends
no dirty, ragged seams

**NATHANIEL:** But those sweet days are gone
I see them only in my dreams.

**NIPSY:**    What lies ahead I do not know, but
come what may, I'll cope.

**DOMINIC:**    I won't give up my vision
I will not lose my hope.

**MUSTAPHA:** What keeps me in good spirits?
My confidence is key.

**SLIM:**    I'm getting stronger day by day
and I believe in me.

**ZEB:**    It isn't always easy
to feel so safe and sure.

**COOL B:**    Even now there still are times
when I feel insecure.

**OMAR:**    But with self-love comes power
and with self-knowledge, trust . . .

**ALL:**    Armed with these I cannot fail
I will succeed, I must!

# THE END

# Index